LEADERSHIP CORE

LEADERSHIP
CORE

CHARACTER, COMPETENCE, CAPACITY

DICK DANIELS
THE LEADERSHIP DEVELOPMENT GROUP

What People Are Saying About *Leadership Core*

◆

"*Leadership Core* will help you develop both your character and competence. This will not only help you become a better leader; it will help you become a better human being!"
—MARSHALL GOLDSMITH, *Thinkers 50 Award, #1 Leadership Thinker in the World, La Jolla, California*

"I once thought that being a true leader was only possible for those born with intrinsic leadership skills – they simply 'were' great leaders, they hadn't needed to work to 'become' such. For any others trying to become great leaders, the effort could be likened to the elusive chasing after the wind. Thankfully, that way of thinking is quite far from reality. Leadership coaches like Dr. Dick Daniels help cultivate effective and true leaders out of desiring subjects who possess (or have a willingness to possess) core ingredients and essential character. Dr. D's books and leadership insights reveal the pathway to genuine, brilliant leadership – a journey where the ordinary becomes extraordinary."
—KRISTI UHLAND, *Community Relations, Lifework Leadership, Ponte Vedra, Florida*

"I have known Dick Daniels for two decades. His voice is timeless, inspiring our African roots to align with relevant leadership that matters. His voice is much needed in this time of crisis where hard choices need to be made, and honest, empathetic clear leadership is needed. Daniels advocates true leadership as a project of hope rather than a crisis to manage."
—THEO GEYSER, PhD, *InVia, Cape Town, South Africa*

"I have always admired great leaders in both business and ministry. Entrepreneurial by nature, I have been a leader in both of those arenas. Unfortunately, my God-given aptitudes do not include natural leadership skills. So, I have needed help to learn leadership. In *Leadership Core*, Dick Daniels offers the kind of leadership skills individuals like me need."
—STEVE SAINT, *Founder, www.itecusa.org, Indigenous Technology and Education Center, Dunnellon, Florida*

"Dick Daniels is an experienced leader who draws from the rich experience of his work. Daniels has the unique ability to make complex, sophisticated business theory both accessible and applicable to leaders who want to be smart in their work and grow as a person. I have referred many of my coaching clients to Daniels' books for a "briefing" in areas that are pressing to leaders in the field."
—DR. DAVID GALLOWAY, *Galloway Consulting, Atlanta, Georgia*

"*Leadership Core* is a brilliant collection of leadership lessons typically learned the hard way, expertly written by Dr. Daniels, and assembled in a very readable format. This book is an essential resource for leaders faced with lighting the path in an unprecedented landscape of uncertainty. Now more than ever, anyone in a leadership role simply must read this book."
—ANGIE BRAINARD, *EVP Talent Management, Right Management Florida/Caribbean*

"When I grow up, I want to write and think like Dr. Dick Daniels! Pick any topic in this wisdom-filled book and—before you read the chapter—list your bullet points on the subject. Trust me, Dick will enlarge and enrich your list. He goes both deep and wide on issues that matter. I'm recommending this gem to both emerging leaders and savvy, street-smart leaders. Trust me— *Leadership Core* will be your book-of-the-year."
—JOHN PEARSON, *Board Governance & Management Consultant, John Pearson Associates, Inc., San Clemente, California*

"I'm delighted to recommend Dick Daniels' new book, *Leadership Core*. We have been good friends for many years—through easy times and also very challenging ones. To highlight his work in leadership, I would say: (1) He is always honest, doing the very best for all within his reach. (2) His new book is practical, current, and creative. (3) This book can be used in a wide variety of ways and for a broad array of people. (4) Daniels' history of leading shines through the mixture of topics and unique ways of presenting solid ideas."
—DR. PENNY ZETTLER, *Retired Minister, St Paul's Methodist Church, Mendota Heights, Edina, Minnesota*

"Everyone wants to change the world, but nobody wants to change themselves. Dick Daniels reminds us that we need leaders who not only know what to do but also know who they are. His focus on both character and competence is the pathway for effective leadership and has never been needed more!"
—TIM PERRIER, *Chaplain, Florida House of Representatives, Tallahassee, Florida*

"Dr. Daniels got it right! Leaders need to pay attention to both sides of leadership...the relational side AND the results side. It all starts and ends with Trust!"
—DAVID HORSAGER, *Founder and CEO, Trust Edge Leadership Institute, St. Paul, Minnesota*

"*Leadership Core* is an essential handbook on leadership! Dick has done the hard work of taking decades of leadership expertise and condensing it into a valuable resource for leaders at all levels. Leadership is not just about what you do, it is about who you are, and *Leadership Core* is a challenging and provocative guide."
—LISA BISHOP, *Coach, Trainer, and Founder of Leadership Unleashed and the podcast, Living a Life Unleashed, Chicago, Illinois*

"Dick Daniels is an expert in organizational strategy. In this book, he outlines the keys to effective leadership and the importance of integrity, character, and competence to lead personally, interpersonally, and ultimately, organizationally. This guide will help leaders hone their skills as well as build new leaders in their organizations."
—WAYNE COOPER, *Executive Chairman, Chief Executive Group, Greenwich, Connecticut*

"Character, competency, and capacity are the leadership trifecta, and Dr. Dick Daniels connects the dots for leaders. Especially in an era where leadership character can seem in short supply, this thoughtful piece will help establish a strong, three-legged foundation for leaders to influence and impact others."
—KRISTIN EVENSON, *Consultant and Executive Coach, Junctures LLC, Minneapolis, Minnesota*

"I had the marvelous opportunity to meet Dick Daniels at an Association for Talent Development (ATD) conference hosted at the Yale School of Management on the campus of Yale University. Dr. Daniels was moderator for a panel in one of the sessions. I was impressed by his leadership approach in the journey of discovering your leadership potential and the right tools to unleash your organizational effectiveness. One of the most important things I learned from him is to focus on what is important in the organization: the culture, the people, and the right leadership. The strategy will follow! *Leadership Core* will guide you on that same journey."
—ELIZA QUINONES NIULKA, *Human Resource Director, Foundation for Puerto Rico, Guaynabo, Puerto Rico*

"I have been reading the Leadership Development eLetter for years and built up a wonderful virtual relationship with Dick Daniels. He is flexible, smart, and eager for discovery. Those qualities shine in everything he's written."
—MAC BOGERT, *President, AzaLearning, Annapolis, Maryland*

"How can you excel in today's VUCA and pandemic landscape? Read *Leadership Core*. Dick uses limited words to generate a myriad of precious insights for effective and ethical leadership crucial for our days. He shows ways of healthy and sustainable leadership that stretch personal, interpersonal, and organizational leadership potential. I am convinced that this book will assist in connecting ethical values with best practices in personal and organizational leadership across all sectors of society."
—DR. ALEXANDER NEGROV, *Founder and President, Hodos Institute, Seattle, Washington and St. Petersburg, Russia.*

"During a time when society could use a mirror to see its effects, Daniels' book puts the leaders squarely in the center as role models for integrity. Key insights are shared to ensure leaders recognize their role in shaping their organization's culture, which include everything from guiding workforce effectiveness to creating long-lasting customer relationships."
—OLESEA AZEVEDO, *SVP and Chief HR Officer, Advent Health, Altamonte Springs, Florida*

"The entire leadership industry focuses on the why, the what, and the how. I can take the best work of somebody else, but if I have a flawed character, I will never get a fraction of the result. In *Leadership Core*, Dick Daniels addresses the foundational missing piece, that is, who you are as a leader. It starts out with developing your character. And then, it shows how to put that into action and how to do that with others. Thank you so much for writing this book. It is exactly what is needed right now."
—JOHN RAMSTEAD, *CEO, Beyond Influence, Denver, Colorado*

"Daniels' bi-weekly e-mails always bring me an interesting turn to the situations I have encountered in my practice, either directly or indirectly. He always manages to analyze the problem in a very concise and interesting way."
—DR. RENATA KAPITANOVA, *Czech Republic*

"In *Leadership Core*, Dick Daniels has succinctly captured the challenges that leaders must address in today's organizations. The ability to recognize rapidly changing requirements and take appropriate action, demands a new approach that combines hard and soft skills. Daniels presents this in a format you will find compelling. I heartedly recommend this book and its timely approach."
—LARRY SHOEMAKER, *President, Cornerstone International Group, Atlanta, Georgia*

"Dick Daniels' insightful approach to leadership makes it easy for new leaders, seasoned leaders, and aspiring leaders to understand and implement practices, behaviors, and mindsets for positive influence on oneself and others!"
—NIRANJANI CHIDAMBER PAPAVARITIS, *Project Manager, Healthcare Content, The Association of Talent Development (ATD), Alexandria, Virginia*

"A few years back, I asked Hall of Fame coach, Joe Gibbs, with whom I had the privilege of working, how he determined player selection in the NFL draft and free-agent process. His strategy was simple and clear in order of priority 1) character, 2) football smarts/ understanding, and 3) athletic ability. Many may assume just the opposite ranking, but it reflects a fascinating alignment with Dick Daniels' new book, *Leadership Core: Character, Competence, Capacity*. In brief and thought-stimulating chapters, Daniels offers immediately applicable lessons for leadership development and change for large and small businesses and nonprofits alike. His thoughtful and tested advice in his bi-weekly Leadership Development eLetter has directly enhanced my own personal leadership. This book is a welcome guide for those seeking to develop dynamic, character-based, competent leadership with increasing levels of responsibility."
—DR. LEE CORDER, *former NFL Chaplain and Senior VP, International Initiatives, Young Life, Washington D.C.*

"If Leadership in action always baffled you, then this book is the key to unlock its mysteries. Dr. Daniels' *Leadership Core: Character, Competence, Capacity* is a practical qualitative approach to leadership with all the core elements to reach a pathway to positive influence and action. Everything that needs to be said about leadership is included in this book. In my twenty-seven years of professional experience, I have never run across a book with a holistic approach which combines ethics and action in pursuit of leadership potential."
—IOANNA BOUSSIA, *Chief Officer Business Planning, Information Technologies and Project Management, City of Penteli, Athens, Greece*

"Dick Daniels has written an inspirational and influential book of reflections, stories, inquiries, and debriefs that capture the essence of leadership character, competence, and capacity for these complex and unpredictable times. Clearly, Daniels is not interested in being the rear guard of leadership. Instead, he is preparing leaders for their future. The book is relevant, authentic, and provides hope for those who have asked, "How/Where/When/Why am I doing this?" It is recommended reading for current and aspiring leaders as well as anyone else who is navigating the perpetual whitewater of leadership – that reflective journey of thinking, communicating, using authority, building relationships, making decisions, and taking action in VUCA and BANI environments. As I did with Daniels' first book, *Leadership Briefs*, I plan to use the content of this book with those I coach, facilitate, and consult through Cultivating Vertical Connections."
—GEORGE F. SHARP, ED.D., *Founder, Cultivating Vertical Connections, Retired Superintendent of Schools, and Former EdD Program Director in the LEAD Program, Stockton University, Millville, New Jersey*

"I am very happy to see that Dick Daniels has provided tools and tough questions that enable leaders to examine their blind spots, their character, and their views of other people in order to reflect upon their readiness and potential effectiveness to be true leaders. Too often leadership books propose leadership styles and approaches without confronting leaders themselves. Polonius's time-tested words to his son in Shakespeare's play Hamlet can be applied to the leader. As he pronounced: "This above all: to thine own self be true." If leaders become aware of their true feelings toward others and are willing to heal negative traits and attitudes, then they are positioning themselves to be authentic leaders who can see and bring out the best in others and open the doors of opportunity for others to become authentic leaders also. Daniels' book provides everything a leader requires in order to lead themselves in order to better lead others. I highly recommend that all leaders follow the journey that Daniels' book lays out."

—RANDAL JOY THOMPSON, PHD, *Co-editor of Leadership and Power in International Development: Navigating the Intersections of Gender, Culture, Context, and Sustainability, Winner of the 2019 R. Wayne Pace HRD Book of the Year Award, Reno, Nevada*

"Dick Daniels has written a book that will challenge you to think about and take action to develop your leadership core. Don't rush to read through the book. Take time to reflect and note your answers to the questions at the end of each chapter. Reading his book forced me to reflect on the "whys" of my current leadership responsibilities, as well as how I am doing with them. Whether you are starting out in your leadership responsibility, or you have been in leadership for some time, this book will challenge you afresh. Additionally, get a copy for your team and use it to coach others."

—FRANCIS BUKACHI, *Executive Director, Hope Alive Initiatives, Nairobi Kenya, Africa*

"Dick Daniels has always offered us down-to-earth, clear, and practical knowledge regarding executive coaching and organizational leadership. Now he brings this added dimension of character and competence to our conversation. As a career educator I am excited to engage with this book as an excellent companion to his previous book, *Leadership Briefs*. This is a timely subject!"

—DR. RICHARD L. GATHRO, CEO, *The Gathro Group, St. Petersburg, Florida*

"All the information in *Leadership Core* is inspiring and educational. A leader has to be a good example to the people they are leading. Leaders need a parental heart of love when making decisions on behalf of their teams."
—BAGUMA NTALE PATRICK, *Director, Omega Orphanage Care Foundation, Kampala, Uganda.*

"Dick Daniels' book speaks to three essential C's of leadership: Character, Competence, and Capacity and how these attributes define a leader. Daniels' style is always focused and brings one to a point of self-reflection and a call to action. An essential read for all leaders."
—SCOTT NYGAARD M.D., *Chief Operating and Medical Officer, Lee Health, Fort Myers, Florida*

"In addition to the many leadership qualities Dick Daniels brings our attention to, I would gladly add one that characterizes him in a very special way: Generosity. Whether it be in the form of the consistent and solid structure of his books, the density of the content of his shared learnings and experiences, or the dedicated presence alongside his clients and friends, Daniels expresses his authentic ambition for one's growth and therefore for our common good. May this read inspire you to go and do the same."
—INES MORTREUIL, *President, Animato, Paris, France*

"Dr. Daniels puts difficult and sometimes vague leadership concepts into concrete challenges and frameworks. It's a book that is much more than any other self-development book filled with shortcuts. There are no shortcuts when it comes to building integrity and character. *Leadership Core* helps the reader through the most challenging parts of a leader's walk."
—LEIF INGVALD SKAUG, *Former CEO Compassion Scandinavia, Mysen, Norway*

ACKNOWLEDGEMENTS

◆

A writing project is always a snapshot in time that reflects the learning, the experiences, and especially the relationships that have influenced the thinking of any author. First of all, I think of all the corporate leaders I have had the opportunity to walk alongside in six to eighteen-month executive coaching engagements for these past twenty years. They have provided insights into industries, corporate cultures, and the real-time challenges of leadership practitioners. My bi-weekly writing in the *Leadership Brief eLetter* has often been in response to the themes I continue to hear regarding leadership dilemmas that need greater clarity.

» In the past three years, I have been privileged to be part of the great Talent Management team at Right Management, Florida and Caribbean. The entire team across Florida has added to my experiences and relationships by providing new understandings of organizational culture and the growing need for leadership development at all levels in every organization. Our Talent Management SVP, **Angie Brainard**, always stretches my enthusiasm and commitment to our craft of executive coaching and team facilitation.

» I have had the opportunity to facilitate peer groups from various industry sectors with the Chief & Senior Executive Network. Their member meetings across the United States bring together CEOs and senior leaders to experience an executive roundtable for discussion on their current business challenges. I have also coached a group of emerging leaders in their Next Level Leader Program. Thanks to **Rob Grabill**, President, Chief and Senior Executive Network, and **Wayne Cooper**, Executive Chairman, Chief Executive Group.

» The EdD program in Organizational Leadership at Stockton University in New Jersey has afforded me an annual opportunity to teach a course on Ethical Leadership. **George Sharp** and **Joe Marchetti** were the designers of one of the most creative EdD programs in Organizational Leadership I have seen. It focuses on their commitment to both vertical and horizonal leadership. **John Gray** is leading that program now, and I have been blessed to experience four cohorts of amazing doctoral students in that program. I don't have enough room to mention each student by name who is leading effectively in their respective communities, primarily throughout New Jersey and Pennsylvania, but I am proud to stay connected with them through LinkedIn and other social media platforms. They are making a difference in the lives of so many!

» The Leadership Development Group is my consulting firm and also the name of the group I host on LinkedIn. The group is now pushing 30,000 global members, half of whom are from outside North America. This online community provides a rich resource of connections to leadership practitioners across every border and at every level of organizational structure. In the past, I hosted a Discussion Topic of the Week. The insights and observations from this group have added to the depth and breadth of my global understanding of leadership and organizational development.

» This year, I was invited to be part of the Student Leadership Forum on Faith and Values open to university students in Florida. Similar events occur across the country as part of the National Student Leadership Forum on Faith and Values which is held annually in Washington, D.C. These events are connected to the vision and mission of the National Prayer Breakfast each February in Washington, D.C. that attracts leaders from 140 countries around the world. The interactions with other facilitators and their groups of students are inspiring as we get a glimpse of the next generation of leaders. **Tim Perrier**, Chaplain, of the Florida House of Representatives leads this initiative, collaborating with **Bill and Grace Nelson** whose vision launched the Florida

Student Forum three decades ago. This event and the people involved with it have inspired me!

» My seven grandchildren inspired the writing of my children's book, *Oak Street Tree House – The Day They Messaged God*, which was just awarded a national book award and two regional book awards. Six of the grands are the characters in the story. They make me laugh and bring me great joy during this season of life. Along with their parents, they give me hope for the world of tomorrow. Thank you: **Annie, Colt, Addi, Cash, Cora, Brit,** and **Cooper**. I am thankful for the leadership insights I see in you, even at a young age! I cannot wait to see how your leadership skills and calling develop as you grow and mature in the years ahead. Thanks to your awesome parents, **Andrea and Jeremy Heckman, Troy and Jessica Daniels, Krista and Adam Saxon**, for putting in the work to shape the unique person and leader each one of you is becoming.

» My leadership sightline has gone global through the invitation to join the Hodos Institute Board of Directors. This group of visionaries is led by founder, **Alexander Negrov**. His passion for leadership development in Eurasia is focused particularly on Ukraine and Russia. Alexander is in the process of translating my book, *Leadership Briefs*, into Russian as a resource his team can use in that part of our world! Joining the board has given me an opportunity to understand the need in this area of the world and contribute to the strategic planning by the board as well as give support to the Hodos staff.

» An earlier writing project was offered through the International Leadership Association. Their annual Building Bridges series included my chapter, "Leadership Musings" in the book, *Leadership and Power in International Development: Navigating the Intersection of Gender, Culture, Context, and Sustainability*. The volume was selected by the Academy of Human Resource Development as their 2019 R. Wayne Pace Book of the Year. It stretched me in the area of international leadership development.

» I have had the unique privilege to volunteer with an awesome team of leaders with Young Life in Southwest Florida. At the recent Leadership Retreat I saw leadership at its best in 36 other staff and volunteers who have a passion to impact the next generation of middle school, high school, and university students. **Courtney Lancaster** and **Miranda Bilello** give senior leadership to the student clubs in this region. I serve in a very minor role with a dozen others in the Young Life Capernaum Club for students with disabilities. **Dale Harris** leads this initiative supported by her husband **Ross Harris** to serve this often overlooked group of amazing young people in our community. I love watching leaders with a vision, mission, and strategy in action.

» I am not a subject matter expert in areas of contemporary technology. I am grateful to **Stephen Datz** who is the Interim Chief Information Officer at Jacksonville Electric Authority in Jacksonville, FL. Stephen is a corporate connection in the work I do throughout Florida and was willing to review Chapter 40 and add invaluable insights into the final manuscript.

» **Heidi Sheard**, thank you for your literary skill in your edits and insight on every page. You have followed my thinking since we worked together on my first book, *Leadership Briefs*. This book has reached a level of writing excellence not otherwise possible because of your involvement.

» **Kendal Marsh**, thank you for your creative touch in designing the cover of both of my leadership books. Your keen sense of design carries through to the interior pages and creates an interesting sensory experience for the reader that goes far beyond black letters on a white page. www.kendalmarsh.com

» A personal word of appreciation to **Marshall Goldsmith**. He is a two-time winner of the Thinkers 50 Award for #1 Leadership Thinker in the World and has been ranked as the #1 Executive Coach in the World as well as a Top Ten Business Thinker for the past eight years. Marshall is the author of thirty-six books including three New York Times Best Sellers. His books have sold 2.5 million copies and are listed as a best seller in twelve countries. His books, *What Got You Here Won't Get You There* and *Triggers* have been recognized by Amazon.com as two of the *100 Best Leadership and Success Books* in their *Read in Your Lifetime* series. Thank you, Marshall, for believing in the need for leaders to develop both character and competence to enhance their leadership capacity and for generously endorsing this book!

So grateful to you all for your encouraging words,

Dr. D…

ISBN: 978-0-578-76418-4

Library of Congress Control Number: 2020918164

Print book first edition

Printed in the United States of America

First Printing 2020-2021

18 17 16 15 19   5 4 3 2 1

Cover and Interior Design: The Brand Office

The Leadership Development Group
Naples, FL
www.theldg.org

CONTENTS

RESPECT: *The Interpersonal Side of Character is What You Think About Other People*

PART TWO: CORE COMPETENCE

CORE COMPETENCE: *The Pathway to Effective Action*

LEADING PERSONALLY: *The Foundation of Competence*

LEADING INTERPERSONALLY: *The Relational Side of Competence*

LEADING ORGANIZATIONALLY: *The Framework of Competence*

PART THREE: CORE CAPACITY

◆

CORE CAPACITY: *The Pathway to Leadership Potential*

PERSONAL DRIVE: *Desire and Effort in Achieving Professional Goals*

WHEN DID YOU LAST INVEST IN YOURSELF?

Why another leadership book? Let me tell you my story. I was leading an organization that I founded out of my entrepreneurial wiring. We did the whole package of management system agendas: vision, mission, values, strategy, structure, and staffing. We trained volunteers, hired staff, designed budgets, created reporting systems, bought property, raised funds, built buildings, and developed leaders. Some of it we did well, some not so well. We kept learning.

The leadership challenges I kept bumping into led to my recognition of my personal need for executive coaching. If I had listened to the wise counsel of others, I might have found a coach much sooner. It stands to reason that we could all use a bit of coaching now and then. Today, as I coach others, I am finding similar organizational and leadership challenges across all industry sectors. My first book, *Leadership Briefs: Shaping Organizational Culture to Stretch Leadership Capacity*, addressed the connection between culture and leadership development. This sequel builds on my continued learning and thinking about culture as the context for what I call the Leadership Core.

My *Leadership Core Matrix* is included in the introduction to this volume. It visually tells the whole story and shows my latest insight in connecting the dots among character, competence, and capacity. When leaders develop their character alongside developing their competence, it enhances their overall leadership capacity. Capacity speaks to our ability and readiness to lead at higher levels of organizational complexity. I write for the leader who is committed to greater effectiveness and efficiency. The leadership theorist, the researcher, or the academic may add insights that go beyond the scope and purpose of my writing, which is meant to be a framework that demystifies the ways in which organizations can expand and deepen the potential of their leadership resources.

At the end of each chapter, you will find a brief summary, The Core, followed by a reflection question that emerged from that chapter. The often-missing step between learning and development as a leader is the pause for reflection. It is the necessary but often overlooked process for meaningful application, so be sure and take time for this. Reflection lends itself to valuable scenario thinking. Be sure to keep asking how the key concepts in a chapter apply to your leadership situation. What new habits might you need to form and implement?

So, when did you last invest in *yourself* to get up to speed on what's required in your current role or what you'll need for your next move, forward or up?

Learning and Leading with You,

Dr. D
www.theLDG.org

Those who bring leadership order out of organizational chaos and those who bring leadership insight into organizational capacity are equipped to lead for the long haul.

Leadership development is contextual, and organizational culture is the context in which leaders develop. The healthier the organization, the more effective the leader. The healthier the leader, the more effective the organization.

THE COMPANY'S STORY

THE INDIVIDUAL'S STORY

◆

THE COMPANY'S STORY: ORGANIZATIONS ARE ALWAYS DEVELOPING

Organizational Development research and literature describe the normal and predictable stages of development and deterioration that any organization will experience as part of the organizational story. The leadership challenge is knowing when to step back and reflect on the sequence in that developing story. Vision leads to mission. Mission leads to strategy. Strategy leads to structure. Structure leads to staffing. Staffing leads to systems. This sequence is both dynamic and linear at the same time. Think of it in reverse order. Systems are the result of staffing. Staffing is the result of structure. Structure is the result of strategy. Strategy is the result of mission. Mission is the result of vision. Vision, mission, and values rarely, if ever, change, but everything else in the sequence keeps changing dynamically. If leaders do not anticipate the normal and predictable challenges in each stage of organizational development, then ignoring needed changes in the strategy, structure, staffing, and systems will eventually contribute to organizational atrophy and ineffectiveness.

The task of leadership is to step up to that lonely place that offers a 30,000-foot perspective to see what others do not yet see. Yes, leaders must step away from operations to find the uninterrupted time and a place to do the groundwork of strategy. If they don't, no one else will except their competition. When leaders see around the corner what others do not yet see, they are gaining perspective to identify and collect the most relevant data needed to plan for success. They are investing in the higher order thinking tasks of analysis and synthesis.

> » ANALYSIS. It's important to collect and understand the data about the industry, market, product line, customer, competition, investors, and employment team. That is the work of analysis. Some will need help in that task from team members gifted with analytical skills, training, and experience. Regardless of how that work gets done, someone needs to take responsibility to analyze the brutal realities of where the organization is today. There will often be good, bad, and ugly parts to that story.

> » SYNTHESIS. Step two is the journey of connecting the dots from the current reality to a preferred or necessary future state. Leaders initiate change in organizations to keep the company from hunkering down and settling for past performance with an assumption that nothing in the industry, market, product line, customer, competition, technology, investors, or their employment team has changed. Honest analysis often gives advanced warning of the trendline story: The way we have worked to date will not sustain our development as an organization. Unless we act intentionally, we are headed toward organizational atrophy and deterioration.

BEHIND THE BOARDROOM'S CLOSED DOORS

Two factors that affect organizational development and organizational health are always in the sightline of effective leaders. *The Culture-Climate Values Grid*© is simple to explain but far from simple to lead and manage. Organizations need both leaders and managers. The two terms are different functions of organizational life. The late Peter Drucker, management consultant and author, said it well: "Management is doing things right. Leadership is doing the right things." Oversimplifying the two roles, managers attend to operations and leaders create strategy. Companies have both distinct roles, but in real time, leaders still do some managing and managers still do some leading. Leaders often define the culture (the ideal), while managers are generally on the front line of work where the climate (the real) is shaped. Consider the relationship between culture and climate. Take it a step further and consider where your company's values might enter the equation. How do your values influence the culture and the climate?

THE CULTURE-CLIMATE VALUES GRID

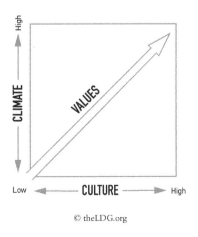

© theLDG.org

CONNECTING THE DOTS

CULTURE describes the values-driven ideal of how team members at all levels of employment are expected to work together in achieving strategic business outcomes. Everything in organizational culture cannot be important at the same time. Values help prioritize a collaboration of ideals.

VALUES define the culture. They prioritize what a company thinks is nonnegotiable in describing how work gets done. It's about how we choose to work together internally as well as how we relate to our vendors and customers externally. Leaders create that ideal picture of organizational culture by articulating a unique mosaic of organizational values. In the sequence of how organizations develop, values are not just *ideas* to believe but *behaviors* to be demonstrated in daily work life.

CLIMATE is the honest assessment of how consistently every employee lives out those values on a daily basis. The culture gap measures the distance between the ideal and the real. It varies moment by moment in every team and every department throughout the entire company. Closing the gap between *culture* and *climate* is an often-hidden challenge of leadership. The gap widens when any of the following realities affect workplace civility:

> » PERSONAL BAGGAGE. This includes issues specific to various seasons of life, such as sleepless nights with infants and toddlers, the exasperation of meeting the needs and demands of aging parents, as well as physical, financial, or relational challenges that blindside us unexpectedly. When we carry the stress of our personal baggage to work, it can impact how consistently and how well we live out the values of our organizational culture.

» PROFESSIONAL DYSFUNCTION. The team's chemistry quotient extends the gap further with every attitude, word, or action that lacks interpersonal savvy in navigating workplace relationships.

» POLITICAL MISSTEPS. The existence of organizational politics occurs when an individual is climbing the hierarchy at any cost. Politics also emerge as teams compete for limited resources in budgeting allocations. Every organization I know would say that they function with limited resources, so politics, in one form or another, are always at play.

» ADOPTION OF VISION, VALUES, AND STRATEGY. When implemented well, this can lead to employee loyalty. However, when there is a shortfall of commitment to the direction set by senior leadership, cynicism and toxic attitudes can lead to broad-scale disengagement.

CLOSING THE GAP BETWEEN CULTURE AND CLIMATE

"BEHAVIORALIZE" THE VALUES. Values are not ideas to believe but behaviors to live. In the world of Organizational Development, values represent the individual and interpersonal attitudes, words, and actions to be demonstrated in daily work life. Truth be told, attitudes lead to words, spoken or unspoken, and words lead to actions. In training sessions, I frequently use an exercise called The List of Ten. The active learning assignment is to list ten words that describe the kind of people you want to live next door to, work alongside, marry into your family, and influence your grandkids. What I have discovered is that words describing positive character are almost universally shared across borders and cultures. A word consistently identified in this exercise is respect. People want to hang around others who are respectful. Though most would agree with this, what does respect look like in daily life in our diverse world?

The second part of the assignment asks the questions: If you were to be a respectful leader, what would you always do? What would you never do? Answering those questions identifies a cluster of behaviors describing a person who treats others with respect. See if you have things to add to this common list of answers: never interrupt, listen, greet everyone, don't play favorites, treat others fairly, be kind and considerate, and follow the Golden Rule. In brainstorming those "always/never" ideas, you have the material needed to "behavioralize" the value. Doing so creates a shared picture of what that value looks like in workplace relationships. That process moves a value from just being an idea that I think about to something that I do throughout my workday when relating to team members, vendors, customers, even the UPS, FedEx, or USPS driver.

SHARE IMMEDIATE FEEDBACK. Each value picture provides the baseline of expectation. It is part of the culture of how we work together and treat each other. When someone from your team keeps interrupting others, you have a behavioral picture to hold them accountable while you give them immediate feedback after the meeting.

Feedback should unfold in three steps – Concern, Impact, and Recommendation: (1) "I'm *concerned* about something I just observed: You interrupted the team several times when they shared an idea you did not agree with." (2) "This is the *impact* I noticed it had on the team: Your comments shut down all the energy in the room. Everyone backed away from engaging in more discussion." (3) "This is my *recommendation* going forward, and I'm sure you will agree: Listen until the other person is actually done talking.

Listen for understanding not for your agreement or disagreement. Listen so you could repeat their idea in your own words. Work deliberately on this, and it will become second nature in no time!" Even though this is quite direct, it does not embarrass them in front of others. It takes them back to the picture of your company culture you all created and agreed to, which is defined by your shared values and illustrated in your *always/never* behaviors.

COMMIT TO CONSISTENT ACCOUNTABILITY. Nothing disengages a team like the star performer who plays by a different set of rules than everyone else. Accountability to the behaviors that reflect the values and define the culture must be consistent across the board. Top performers who get by with what others don't get by with destroy trust within the team as well as negatively affecting future team performance. The critical word is "consistent." Patrick Lencioni adds insight as he builds his pyramid in *The Five Dysfunctions of a Team: A Leadership Fable.* Organizational and team health is based on the foundation of trust, because without it, a team cannot have healthy conflict. Consistent accountability by the leader contributes to a culture of trust and reduces interpersonal dysfunction.

THE INDIVIDUAL'S STORY: LEADERS ARE ALWAYS DEVELOPING

It's a relatively uncomplicated formula. Leaders who are lifelong learners continue to develop their leadership skill set in two areas: character and competence. The dual track of development impacts their capacity as a leader. Remember, capacity is a leader's ability and readiness to lead at higher levels of organizational complexity. If you want to lead more effectively and efficiently in your current role, then address both. If you want to move up the corporate ladder, then develop further in your character and never stop growing in your competence. Some leaders will default to primarily working on their leadership competence. People respect them because of their effectiveness and knowledge in the field, but the shortage of work on their character is often costly in people's perception of who they are.

The other mistake people make is the drive to be liked by everyone else. These leaders develop character but minimize sharpening their skill set of leadership competence. Teams like their leader at first but eventually lose respect because they don't get to the stated results. *The Leadership Character-Competency Grid* below tells a story of the two areas where leaders need continual growth and attention. Developing in the area of leadership character impacts one's Positive Influence in workplace interpersonal relationships. Investing in the development of leadership competency impacts Effective Action in achieving strategic goals.

Leadership Character	Gets at who you are	Tied to Organizational Culture	All About Values	Soft Skills of Leadership	Impacts Relationships	Positive Influence
Leadership Competence	Gets at what you do	Tied to the Bottom Line	All About Strategy	Hard Skills of Leadership	Impacts Results	Effective Action

© theLDG.org

POSITIVE INFLUENCE + EFFECTIVE ACTION = LEADERSHIP CAPACITY

CONNECTING THE DOTS

The Culture Cube provides another visual to represent the connections among character, competence, and capacity. Intentional development in one's character and competence continually enhances, increases, or expands one's leadership capacity. When a leader addresses character more than competence or competence more than character, the *Culture Cube* is distorted. When a leader invests in developing both simultaneously, it models the power of positive influence alongside effective action for every team in the company. As a result, the *Culture Cube* continues to grow and expand to maximize the productive potential of the organization in each stage of organizational development.

THE CULTURE CUBE

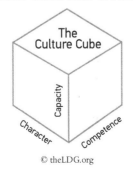

© theLDG.org

CHARACTER – THE CONSISTENCY OF WHO YOU ARE IN PUBLIC AND IN PRIVATE. It represents the soft skills of leading that reflect who you are when everyone is looking and especially when no one is looking. Character brings forward the values that define the culture. It touches the interpersonal side of work life in all the relationships necessary to reach strategic outcomes. Character is evidenced in one's positive influence. Influence can be forced on others because of your title or position, but it will not be perceived positively, and it will not be effectively sustainable.

COMPETENCE – THE EFFECTIVENESS AND EFFICIENCY IN USING THE SKILLS REQUIRED FOR YOUR JOB. It includes the hard skills in the toolbox of leading. Rather than demonstrating who you are, it shows what you do. These skills are tied more to the bottom line than to the culture. Competence connects directly to strategy and results. At the end of the day, one's competence is seen in effective action. Competence development is also critical to leadership sustainability.

CAPACITY – YOUR ABILITY AND READINESS TO LEAD AT HIGHER LEVELS OF ORGANIZATIONAL RESPONSIBILITY. It is the return on investment from continued growth of one's character and competence. Capacity is the ability to lead effectively and efficiently in your current role and the readiness to be considered for opportunities at higher levels of organizational complexity. In certain seasons of life, we may have the capacity to lead at a higher level, but we may not have the readiness to take on more just now. Capacity is the preparedness for an opportunity. Readiness is having the bandwidth in one's life to take advantage of that opportunity. Careers are all about seasons, and each season has transitions that demand different things of us. All seasons are not equal, and each season may not be the time to take on greater responsibility.

The Leadership Core Matrix

Character + Competence = Capacity

LEADERSHIP FOCUS	LEADERSHIP GOAL	LEADERSHIP DEFINITION	LEADERSHIP QUALITY	LEADERSHIP MODEL	LEADERSHIP ACTION	LEADERSHIP SELF-UNDERSTANDING	LEADERSHIP QUESTION	LEADERSHIP INSIGHTS	LEADERSHIP APPLICATION	LEADERSHIP RESULTS
Character										
Leading yourself	Be authentic	Influence of my positive character	Consistency of my leadership behavior	*Being* How leadership is approached	My leadership presence	Who am I?	Do people like me?	Integrity of who I am when everyone is looking and when no one is looking	What behaviors are essential in my leadership practice?	Positive character crosses borders, cultures, genders, and generations
Competence										
Leading others	Be wise	Impact of my effective action	Expertise of my leadership skill	*Doing* What leadership accomplishes	My leadership performance	How good am I?	Do people respect me?	Leadership competence is defined by context, culture, and strategic outcomes	What competencies are critical in my leadership execution?	Aligning my leadership competency mix to the current or anticipated stage of organizational development
Capacity										
Leading the organization	Be strategic	Boundaries of my leadership ability	Depth of my leadership strength	*Knowing* Why leadership succeeds	My leadership potential	How high can I lead?	Do people trust me?	Capacity in one context does not automatically transfer to a different context	What gaps exist that need to be addressed with a leadership coach to enhance my leadership potential?	Awareness of my season of life situational factors that may limit my current ability to lead at a higher level of organizational complexity

When organizational culture only values the bottom line, three things result: (1) Leadership Competency is rewarded, (2) Leadership Character is assumed, and (3) Leadership Capacity is never fully realized.

PART ONE

CORE CHARACTER

Not something to do, but someone to be.

CHARACTER MULTIPLIER #1: INTEGRITY

CHARACTER MULTIPLIER #2: RESPECT

CORE CHARACTER: THE PATHWAY TO POSITIVE INFLUENCE

* * * ◆ * * *

Power in organizations is the capacity generated by relationships.

—MARGARET WHEATLEY
American Author & Management Consultant

◆

THE SHADOW SIDE OF CHARACTER: IS HONESTY THE BEST POLICY?

A measurable aspect of one's character is honesty. It touches so many other qualities of positive character. Honesty influences trust, respect, and loyalty while dishonesty damages those same aspects of interpersonal relationships, both at work and at home. Author, Dr. Tessa West, Associate Professor of Psychology at New York University, reported the impact of *The Lies We Tell at Work — and the Damage They Do.*[1] What she found is that dishonesty shows up in five areas of work:

1. LYING TO LAND A JOB – Lying can show up before you even have the job. Resumé padding can result in hiring people who don't really have the training, experience, or skills for the job.

2. LYING TO GET AHEAD – People lie to get a raise. They take credit for what someone else did or said, and they lie to cover up mistakes.

3. LYING TO ACHIEVE WORK-LIFE BALANCE – People work when they claim to be taking time off, and people take

time off when they claim to be working. Both are damaging.

4. LYING WITH FEEDBACK – Many leaders and managers are not trained in how to give effective feedback, and so they avoid telling the harsh truth in a feedback conversation with direct reports. A too-nice culture creates an environment where team members who need to improve have no idea in what areas and how.

5. LYING DURING THE EXIT INTERVIEW – People often say they are leaving for more money, but it may not be true. People leave because of their boss but are afraid to be honest about it because they fear retribution in future references or recommendations. Some no longer care. The result is that companies rarely identify the actual reasons people leave.

Dr. West discovered that people lie more on Monday and Friday than Tuesday, Wednesday, or Thursday. We can intuitively understand why that is! She also found that most people lie two to four times a day. She says, "Most of the lies we tell feel harmless. But the consequences are far from it. Dishonesty can kill healthy team dynamics, encourage manipulation and deception, and keep honest people from getting ahead. What's more, the habit of telling lies, even little ones, is contagious. It doesn't take long for a habit to become a norm, and a norm to become a culture."

Honesty provides a glimpse into one's character. Dr. West's research gives one example of the shadow side that illustrates what the lack of character can do to organizational life. People use lies to avoid difficult situations or hide what they are really feeling or what they are intending to do. Lying always comes with a price, and honesty has its rewards.

» As my Mom said often, "Be sure your sins will find you out." It's true. The truth will eventually come out, and when it does the original situation is only worse.

» It contributes to your own sense of integrity and the trust factor in all your relationships.

» When you lie, you are caught in a trap of trying to remember what you told to whom.

» Owning honesty teaches you how to deal with difficult situations that are part of life.

What about the other side to this story? What is the impact on organizations when leaders are recognized as people of positive character?

THE ORGANIZATIONAL ROI: THE CASE FOR CHARACTER-BASED LEADERSHIP

In strategizing the most expedient way to address the bottom line and profitability for investors, it is tempting to look for shortcuts and loopholes to give competitive advantage in the marketplace. Fred Kiel ran the numbers in statistical research over seven years to document the return on investment when character is front and center in corporate life. His study, as discussed in his book, *Return on Character: The Real Reason Leaders and Their Companies Win*, involved 8000 employees, 100 CEOs, and their executive teams at Fortune 500 and 100 companies, privately held firms, and nonprofits. The research gave insight into public documents, behavior, and performance by leaders.[2] In his book, Kiel reported results showing that CEOs of high integrity generate superior financial returns.

The CEOs in the study allowed Kiel to survey a sampling within their companies of what employees thought about their most senior leader. He discovered that leaders of high character demonstrated integrity, compassion, and accountability. They brought shareholders five times as much profit as their lower scoring, self-absorbed colleagues. In his study, the self-focused leaders with the lowest scores were most concerned about prominence in the business community and their own financial success. They saw employees as replaceable human capital, not as people. In his interviews with this group, he found them to be lonely, pessimistic, distrustful, sometimes combative, and overall, less willing to learn and grow.

Character is that unique blend of values, beliefs, and habits that influence both how an individual responds to life situations and also how they relate to the people in those situations. I will always remember the statement from Frances Hesselbein, former CEO of Girl Scouts of the USA, published in an online article with *Investor's Business Daily* called "Quiet Revolutionary Frances Hesselbein Makes Leadership Her Mission"[3] She is now 103 years old at the time of this writing, and she said it well: "Leadership flows from inner character and integrity of ambition, which inspires others to lend themselves to your organization's mission."

The HOW Institute for Society "builds and nurtures a culture of moral leadership, principled decision-making, and values-based behavior that enables individuals and institutions to meet the profound social, economic, and technological changes of the 21st century to elevate humanity." Their newest report titled, "The State of Moral Leadership in Business 2020" includes data from 1500 individuals working in the business sector. These are some of the findings. You can read more in more detail at www.thehowinstitute.org.[4]

> » 86% say the need for moral leadership is more urgent than ever.

> » 74% say their colleagues would do a better job if their managers relied more on moral authority than formal power (title and position).

> » 79% say their organizations would make better business decisions if they followed the Golden Rule.

> » 46% say they would take a pay cut to work for a moral leader.

> » The respondents indicated that only 7% of managers and 8% of CEOs consistently demonstrate moral leadership behaviors in the highest tier of leaders in this study.

Respondents who report to managers demonstrating consistent moral leadership are more likely to rate their organizations highly on key performance indicators (KPIs) compared to those with managers at the lowest tier of moral leadership behaviors. Seventy percent of managers in the top tier of moral leadership say that their company is oriented to long-term metrics rather than short-term metrics while only 11% with managers at the lower tier of moral leadership assert that perspective. Other comparisons between the highest and lowest tiers of moral leadership include:

» Five times more likely to report that their company has satisfied customers.

» Seven times more likely to expect improved business results in the coming year.

» Thirteen times more likely to see their company as highly adaptable to change.

An encouraging finding in the HOW research is that 77% believe that people can develop moral leadership behaviors. So, how do we develop moral leaders of character who lead with positive influence?

Moral leadership behaviors are demonstrated interpersonally. There is a resource that I assign in almost every executive coaching engagement. The book is from the Arbinger Institute and titled, *Leadership and Self-Deception: Getting Out of the Box.*[5] It takes a deep dive into the premise that positive character is connected to how an individual relates to others, using the metaphor of leading inside or outside the box. When leaders stay inside the box, they see others as their support team who work to make them look good. In Chapter Ten of *Leadership Core,* "Hierarchical Elitism," I describe those who lead from inside the box. But, when a leader chooses to lead outside the box, it levels the hierarchy and flattens the organization. In leading outside the box, leaders see their role as doing everything possible to make each team member successful. That is servant leadership. It demonstrates the behavior of moral leadership at its most foundational level. Leaders accomplish out of the box leading by coaching team members and investing in their development to extend their leadership capacity. It's a leadership style that aligns positive influence with effective action or leadership character with leadership competence. The first part of my leadership formula is described in detail in this first section in *Leadership Core*. So how does one develop a consistency of moral character that leads to positive influence? Two character multipliers provide a guide for the well-intended leader: Integrity (Chapters 1-7) and Respect (Chapters 8-14).

Commitments organize the hours and the days of a life. A committed person achieves consistency across time. His character is built through the habitual acts of service to the people he loves. His character is built by being the humble recipient of other people's gifts and thus acknowledging his own dependency. A contract gets you benefits, but a commitment transforms who you are.

—DAVID BROOKS
The Second Mountain: The Quest for a Moral Life

CHARACTER MULTIPLIER #1

Integrity: The Personal Side of Character is What Other People Think About You

Make us to choose the harder right instead of the easier wrong and never to be content with a half truth when the whole can be won.

—FROM THE CADET PRAYER

The United States Military Academy at West Point

THE JOHARI WINDOW 360: BLIND SPOTS

The Johari Window is a sociological matrix that gives people insight into self-perceptions and the perceptions of other people. We say perceptions become reality, but what happens when our self-perception clashes with how others see us? In 1955 psychologists, Joseph Luft and Harrington Ingram created the Johari Window using their first names as the basis for the name of their construct. Joseph Luft wrote a book about the subject in 1969 called *Of Human Interaction: The Johari Model.*

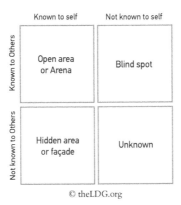

© theLDG.org

The Johari Window Model

THE OPEN AREA – Information about your attitudes, behavior, emotions, habits, mannerisms, feelings, skills, and views will be known by other people as well as by yourself. The goal is not to have an enlarged open area with anyone or with everyone. There is strength and benefit when you live with a large open area with a few people who know you well and offer unconditional love and acceptance along with their honest and constructive feedback.

THE HIDDEN AREA – Information known to you but not to others. It includes past events, experiences, fears, secrets, mistakes, and failures. We keep this information to ourselves because we are not sure what others may think of us if they knew, and then we may fear what others might do with that information.

THE UNKNOWN AREA – Information which we are not aware of, nor are others, related to our interests, strengths, capabilities, talents, etc. We may not yet have training or experience to introduce us to certain things, and it's important to recognize that. Expanding our networks can lead to new insights and new opportunities in areas we have interest or aptitude.

THE BLIND SPOTS – Information about yourself that others observe but you are unaware of. This includes mannerisms, habits, words overused or used incorrectly, a lack of emotional and social intelligence, offensive behaviors, and political incorrectness. Blind Spots can complicate interpersonal relationships as people hesitate to give us honest feedback.

The four panes in the window are never equal in size, and each pane represents a percentage of the totality of who we are in each relationship at any given moment in time. We can enlarge the Open Area of the Johari Window by reducing the size of the

Hidden Area and the Blind Spots. To reduce the Hidden Area implies that you are willing to be courageously vulnerable by giving people feedback about the things you know about yourself that they are not aware of. Again, the guideline is to work toward a larger Open Area with trusted people in your life. Reducing the size of your Blind Spots necessitates asking people for feedback. It is the moment of truth when you genuinely ask and willingly receive that feedback. Gaining that insight into your Blind Spots can quite literally blindside you both mentally and emotionally. This is the "bull in the china shop" information that makes you dangerous in your working relationships. To grow in these areas requires a willingness to ask. In the corporate world, we provide the opportunity for structured feedback in a 360-degree tool either online or by interview. I always use these four basic questions to get feedback from a leader's direct reports, peers, and senior leaders regarding leadership behaviors or leadership competencies:

1. What does this person do well in leading that they should continue to do?

2. What do they do a good job of, but their role requires them to move from good to great?

3. What are their blind spots that get in the way of their effectiveness and efficiency? Things they should stop doing?

4. What don't they do that they should start doing to be more effective in their role?

Feedback can reveal how you are being perceived in the leadership behaviors reflecting your character. Perceptions influence what others think about you as a person and as a leader. If you want to develop your character, find a way to get credible feedback from a trusted group of work associates who understand that you want to continually learn and develop so you can enhance your positive influence (character) and your effective action (competence).

THE CORE

Blind Spots get in the way of your leadership effectiveness and efficiency, and the only way to identify them is to ask others for feedback. Leaders who have the courage to be vulnerable by asking, listening, and responding are investing in the ongoing development of leadership character that leads to positive influence in work relationships.

REFLECTION QUESTIONS: Who will you ask to give you honest feedback about your Blind Spots? When?

THE LEADER'S REPUTATION: WHEN INTEGRITY ISN'T EASY

Integrity is what others see in you. Respect is what you see in others. Integrity in the context of an organization is tied to modeling the corporate values with consistency when everyone is looking and also when no one is looking. Integrity is the reliability of your attitudes, words, and behaviors.

- Attitude is the mindset you bring into situations regarding people and circumstances.

- Words are the verbal expressions of those attitudes spoken publicly or privately.

- Behaviors are the active expressions of your attitudes and words.

Integrity is what others see in you when they sense your attitudes, hear your words, or observe your behavior. The trust and respect of team members is always tied to the leader's integrity and results in one's positive influence within the team. Qualities of a person of integrity include: honest, principled, virtuous, reliable, consistent, and moral. Qualities of a person who lacks integrity include: deceitful, corrupt, dishonest, inconsistent, and prone to duplicity.

Organizational culture can be the testing ground of integrity as you navigate unpredictable, relational, and political landmines. The attitudes, words, and behaviors of others elicit normal emotional responses that can trigger personality clashes. Emotions come with the mad, sad, glad, afraid, or ashamed moments of work life under the microscope of your entire team. The full repertoire of emotions is enriched with various levels of intensity. For example, anger can be accompanied with frustration (low intensity), anger (medium intensity), or rage (high intensity). The level of intensity adds to the complexity of your emotions. A leader of character is always learning how to be an emotionally smart individual!

When you bump into disruptive situations or personalities that trigger emotions, ask two questions:

1. What is the level of intensity you are *feeling* just now: low, medium, or high? Own the emotion and own how intensely you are feeling that emotion.

2. What is the best way to describe how you are *dealing* with that emotion in response to stressful situations and stressful people? Responsiveness is also demonstrated at three levels: (a) Ignoring the feeling implies low responsiveness (b) Acknowledging the feeling represents medium responsiveness (c) Over-Expression of the emotion represents high responsiveness.

The EQ Matrix for leaders describes five styles of feeling and dealing with emotions.

THE EQ MATRIX

THE STUFFER -High Feeling -Low Dealing		**THE EXHIBITIONIST** -High Feeling -High Dealing	

INTENSITY/FEELING — High ... Low

Emotional Maturity

THE STUFFER
-High Feeling
-Low Dealing

THE EXHIBITIONIST
-High Feeling
-High Dealing

THE APATHETIC
-Low Feeling
-Low Dealing

THE COMPLAINER
-Low Feeling
-High Dealing

Low   RESPONSIVENESS/DEALING   High

© theLDG.org

SEVEN ACTIONS TO MANAGE POWERFUL EMOTIONS

1. OWN – Emotions, both positive and negative, are part of being human.

2. ACCEPT – Everyone reacts emotionally to the events of life in two dimensions: intensity (feeling) and responsiveness (dealing).

3. RECOGNIZE – People or situations trigger emotions, either fairly or unfairly.

4. IDENTIFY – This is the intensity with which you express those emotions, feeling numb or overreacting.

5. CONSIDER – Ask yourself why you respond at the level of intensity you do, rational or irrational.

6. DETERMINE – Know if it is appropriate to publicly express an emotion: how, when, where, and to whom?

7. REFLECT – Think about how you have responded at the end of each day, maturely or immaturely.

THE CORE

Emotionally smart leaders will generally outplay their IQ in much of life. IQ may get you a job, but EQ will create sustainability for the long haul. Owning and managing your emotional responses to troubling situations and people is at the heart of leadership character and your integrity in the eyes of others. It either advances your influence or negates that half of my leadership formula:

Positive Influence + Effective Action = Leadership Capacity.

REFLECTION QUESTIONS: Which area do you need to develop further: feeling your emotions or dealing with your emotions? What situations or people trigger intense emotions at work?

HUMBLY SPEAKING: WHO'S THE HERO

Which statement reflects your attitude toward your team: (1) They are following the leader? or (2) You are leading the followers? Do you focus your efforts on how your direct reports support you as the team leader or on how you as the leader support your team? Your answer distinguishes how you think about leadership, and it defines the organizational culture you are shaping.

Twenty years of executive coaching with corporate clients has given me insight into how leaders understand their role. It's often seen as one of many things on their daily To Do list. The time allocated to lead is whatever time is left over after attending to the other areas of responsibility. I am challenging that understanding. I suggest that leadership is everything you do, and your primary assignment as a leader is to make each of your direct reports successful.

Character is modeled by the servant leader who approaches leadership with an attitude of humility. It is out of that core attitude that you know your calling is to serve those you lead. I referred earlier to the insightful volume from the Arbinger Institute: *Leadership and Self-Deception*. The metaphor in the storyline is about leading from inside the box or from outside the box. Those who think the team exists to serve you are leading from inside the box. Those committed to serving their team are leading outside the box. The attitude of humility in leadership provides a quality of personal character in contrast to the overly confident leader who is perceived as arrogant. Jim Collins, author of *Good to Great*, expresses this humility as Level Five Leadership. He says these leaders are ambitious but more for the benefit of their organization than for themselves. As a result, they serve their team and each team member.

The Humility Audit will help you assess how you are being perceived by those you lead. Assess yourself. Then ask a colleague to assess you. Are there any humility gaps in your self-understanding?

THE HUMILITY AUDIT
© www.theLDG.org

Q1 - Are you a lifelong learner or do you know everything you need to know?

Q2 – Are you courageous enough to consistently model humility?

Q3 – If you have strong feelings about something, are you aware that you might be wrong? Is it more important that you are perceived as being right?

Q4 – Do you say "I" more often or "we?"

Q5 – Do you ask more or tell more?

Q6 – Do you trust your team enough to delegate things they could do, knowing they might do it differently or even better?

Q7 – Do you tend to give the credit, and do you tend to take the blame?

Q8 – When people disagree with you, is your first instinct to listen for understanding, considering that you might have something to learn from them?

Q9 - Are you an inclusive leader who embraces a diversity of thinking with various points of view?

Q10 – Who's ultimately the hero, you or your team?

If you always take the recognition then it dimishes the respect and trust needed within your team. If you always give the recognition then it empowers your direct reports and their direct reports to exceed expectations as a high performing team.

THE CORE

How do you see yourself? How do you see your team? Would those closest to you say that you are a person of character who consistently displays an attitude of humility? Humility isn't a weakness when it is genuine. Confidence won't become arrogance when you take time to understand the points of view from those around you.

REFLECTION QUESTIONS: On a continuum from 1 to 10, what are you like? 1 = Humble. 10 = Arrogant. What is one thing you could do that will help you move toward greater humility?

FAILURE: WHERE CHARACTER IS FORGED

In my honest moments of reflection, I admit that I have learned more from my failures than from my successes. Facing failure while going through the tunnel of chaos is when our perseverance builds character! The journey of failure is a lonely road, but it is possible to walk that way and get to a better destination. Our personal and professional lives include the good, the bad, and the ugly. It is an inevitable part of living in a broken world. Failure may result from your own action or because of the action of someone else. There are also moments of failure that are completely out of our control for which no person can be blamed or held responsible.

Failure moments are a part of life. They invite either our reaction or our response. One attitude is reactive, and one is proactive. There is a statement in ancient literature that says, all things can work together for our benefit. It's a choice. Either we allow all things to mature and develop us or things will come back to haunt us or even control us. The opportunity for leaders is to learn as much from our failures as from our successes and to help others do the same. Modeling failure management is an investment in each of your team members and speaks to the depth of your character.

Failure has many labels: bomb, botch, bust, deficit, downfall, false step, faux pas, washout, total loss, train wreck, epic fail, stalemate, flop, loss, misstep, implosion. However you choose to describe it, failure is in every leader's storyline. It can be personal failure, professional failure, or often an intertwining of both. Personal failure quickly touches the professional and likewise, professional failure eventually touches the personal. Consider these ABCs:

» ADDICTION. When something takes over everything else.

» ACTION. The unintended consequences of crossing the line between right and wrong.

» ARROGANCE. Consistent attitudes and words that denigrate others.

» ASSUMPTIONS. Counter-intuitive decisions that prove to be wrong.

» BIAS. When you're unwilling to look at all the facts.

» BLAME. When you try to put your "failure monkey" on someone else's back

» COMPROMISE. When the end didn't justify the means.

» CHAPTER 11. When you misread the market, misunderstood the strategy, or mismanaged the cash flow.

GETTING THROUGH THE
MINEFIELD OF FAILURE

Failure may seem like the end of your leadership. It may lead to some ending, but that does not prevent a new beginning. A "Do Over" always starts with reflection, I firmly believe! Henry Ford said, "Failure is the opportunity to begin again more intelligently."

WHAT WAS I THINKING? Those four words are not a statement but a question to be answered. Answer it honestly when you are coming out of failure, and you will be positioned for a new beginning. If these words are simply a statement of exclamation, "What was I thinking!" then you are apt to experience the failure again in the future.

OWN THE WHAT AND THE WHY. Admit to yourself and others that you failed. Seek help, if needed, to get to the source of the problem. Owning what you did without addressing why you did it misses the root cause. New beginnings are only possible when you own and understand what happened and why.

ACCEPT THE CONSEQUENCES. Unpleasant and embarrassing but, nonetheless, consequences are a part of getting to the other side of failure. Rather than avoid it, justify it, or explain it away, just pay the price and move on with your character forged in new ways that will benefit future leadership.

REDEFINE YOURSELF. Some will forever label you by the failure and never extend the grace they would demand in their own need to start over some day. Personal failures can be more difficult to leave in the past because of the triggers that remind you of the situation. Professional failures can often be mitigated by leaving the company or the city and starting fresh in a new place. It's hard in some industries to move forward unscathed. The situation may follow you in the industry and its tight network of people who all know each other well. The most important thing is to forgive yourself. It's hard to portray confidence when you don't believe in yourself. As you learn your failure lessons, let who you are becoming overshadow who you were in the past. Time is a healer. Your attitude toward failure as a leadership lesson pushes the experience into a different category than we normally think is possible.

RECYCLE THE PAIN. Do not waste the leadership lessons learned during a season of failure! Resist the urge to describe yourself as a victim. Though that may be true, it is an unhealthy mindset. What can you learn from the situation? Share the what and the why with others. Try to help those you lead avoid those same choices. Be ready to stand with those who may also face the lonely road of failing and offer them the chance to begin again. Be their advocate. That is character at its best.

THE CORE

Four lessons can be learned from failure: (1) Create a team culture where failure is expected and allowed as part of the journey to success. (2) Provide a pathway for failure recovery. (3) Discuss the failure with the team or team member. Ask the first "why" of what is behind the failure. Then ask why once again (and again and again) in order to explore cause and effect relationships that underlie what happened. (4) Identify the insights that will help you build on the failure as a step toward success and avoid repeating the same mistake another time. Learning from your failure builds integrity and character in how you see yourself and how others see you.

REFLECTION QUESTION: What was the biggest failure that kept you from a new beginning?

IDENTITY OR REPUTATION: LEADERS WHO CAN BE TRUSTED

Leadership has more to do with reputation than identity. Reputation is the perception others have of you. Identity is your own sense of who you are. Any distance between those two can destroy integrity and trust. So, how is reputation established?

» First impressions are always in play. Fairly or unfairly, perception becomes the reality of what others think about you.

» Perceptions are reinforced based on how you look and how you sound. Verbals and non-verbals tell the full story. It's not your actual words. It's how you communicate and what body language you use that overrides your words.

» Reputation is reinforced by the consistency of your public and private self. Who are you when everyone is looking, and who are you when no one is looking?

Trust is connected to worthy in the English language: trustworthy. A trusted leader is one who is worthy of another's respect. Being trustworthy is an essential aspect of character. It's the consistency in your attitudes, words, and behavior that reinforces your reputation in the eyes of others.

ADDING, SUBTRACTING, DIVIDING, OR MULTIPLYING TRUST

Trust has more to do with the little details of life at work rather than the major ethical crossroads that are monitored by compliance and measured by legality. It takes time to build trust through the day-to-day consistency of your response to the worst and the best that the culture and climate at work can throw at us. The fragile piece of the trust puzzle is that trust can be lost in one careless conversation or one thoughtless action. Emotional Intelligence is simply letting the thinking side of the brain catch up to the feeling side of the brain in your reaction to something said or done by another. What triggers a subtract or divide in your trust quotient in those moments when you act or speak without EQ? Doing things that add to the perception of your trustworthiness is good, but there are multipliers that effectively develop your character while influencing your reputation to others and their trust of you.

MULTIPLIER #1 - HONESTY. Tell the truth and nothing but the truth. Shaping a story with partial truth to protect yourself or to mislead others always backfires at the most inopportune times. Leaders can choose to withhold part of the truth because they do not trust followers with the whole story. If that is the case, then you may not have the right people on the team. Honesty is destroyed in lies, exaggerations, partial truth, deception, and cover ups. When team members know that they can always count on your words to be accurate and complete, they will be engaged followers even when they may not totally agree with you.

MULTIPLIER #2 – COMMITMENTS. Future promises can be made in order to get what you want or need today. Breaking those commitments in the future contributes to the deterioration of trust. Before you make a promise, be certain that you can and will fulfill it. Sometimes the fulfillment needs to be re-negotiated but never forgotten. The promisor needs to initiate the reminders, never the promisee. Set a completion date. Add it to your calendar. Be the reminder to the person to whom the promise was made. Take the lead and initiative in planning for the fulfillment of each promise. If you cannot keep a commitment, then don't offer it as your bargaining chip. Negotiate your need without a pledge, vow, oath, or guarantee of what will be received. People trust leaders who always follow through with their side of an agreement.

MULTIPLIER #3 – TRANSPARENCY. When leaders work with a hidden agenda, a predetermined conclusion, or decisions orchestrated behind closed doors, then trust is an impossible ideal. When leaders deceptively come through the side door of decision making, to give the appearance that everyone had a voice, then skepticism grows. Decisions are made in many ways: (a) Leaders decide, (b) Team consensus decides, (c) Team majority decides, or (d) Final decisions are discussed and delegated to the end user. When leaders need to make the decision, they need to own it, make the decision, explain why, and take responsibility for the outcomes. In either approach, open or closed, we need to put all the information on the table and allow questions to be asked.

When people know the ground rules and the facts involved, they can buy-in to final decisions even if they did not have ownership or influence in the process. Read Jack Stack's *The Great Game of Business* and note his counter-intuitive idea of "open book management."

MULTIPLIER #4 – CLARITY. Leaders who communicate clearly avoid spin, confusing explanations, and wordy answers. Less verbiage allows time for more questions to clarify what is not yet understood, and it accelerates the process. Clarity is simple. When team members are reading between the lines and catching on to the loopholes in carefully crafted rhetoric that is open to interpretation, they are already on the slippery slope of mistrust. Clarity is enhanced by using word pictures, examples, stories, and visuals to unpack the complexity of big ideas. It is the hard work of leadership communication. It is always easier to ramble for thirty minutes than to get to the point in five. Write out your main point (only one), then look for creative but simple ways to reinforce what it means. Read William Strunk and E.B. White's, *The Elements of Style*, and note their idea of omitting needless words in sentences and needless sentences in paragraphs and needless paragraphs in manuscripts.

MULTIPLIER #5 – CONSISTENCY. When every audience, stakeholder, and team member hears the same message, then everyone has a reason to trust once again. With six degrees of relational separation, followers have all the avenues of social media along with private conversations with co-workers to find out who heard what. Inconsistency is toxic. It's all about reputation. When the leader's public self matches the private self, then there is no hypocrisy. Some people give Oscar-worthy performances, but those with an exemplary reputation are trusted every time, regardless of what opponents may try to portray.

Always add or multiply team trust. Never subtract or divide!

THE CORE

Reputation is not about identity or your self-understanding. It has to do with perception of how others see you. People make observations of you and quickly conclude if they like you and if they respect you. They base the conclusion on how you look and how you sound. It may not be fair, but it is reality. Liking you is all about the interpersonal chemistry and common ground. Respecting you is the recognition of your competence in the work being done. Integrity is reinforced when liking you and respecting you are aligned in the perception of others. That is when people will trust you, and trust is the essential ingredient in leadership influence.

REFLECTION QUESTIONS: What do you feel gets in the way of an accurate perception of who you really are? Are people getting an accurate reflection of your character in how you look and how you sound?

6

OWN YOUR ETHICAL CODE: THE POWER OF ADVANCED DECISION MAKING

My behavior is ten times more important in demonstrating leadership character than my words. It's more about what people see than what they hear. Four styles of leaders are pictured in the Ethical Leader Matrix© below:

THE DYSFUNCTIONAL LEADER – No ethical code in either words or behavior (Lower Left)

THE UNINTENTIONAL LEADER – Ethical behavior without ethical words (Upper Left)

THE HYPOCRITICAL LEADER – Ethical words without ethical behavior (Lower Right)

THE ETHICAL LEADER – Ethical words aligned with ethical behavior (Upper Right)

THE ETHICAL LEADER MATRIX

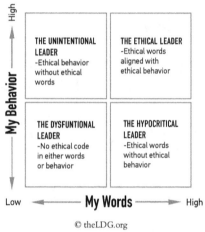

© theLDG.org

A code of ethics is foundational to demonstrating your character as a leader with personal integrity. A code establishes behavioral expectations for your own life and perhaps for your team or company. A personal code is based on the values that guide your behavior when you find yourself in ethical crossroads. It brings clarity to advanced decision making. Even if you want to do the right thing, the right thing is not always clear. At times, the right thing is making the choice between the lesser of two evils. In complex decision making, ethical values and principles may collide.

>> A personal code defines acceptable behavior

>> A personal code is a reference point for self-assessment

>> A personal code provides a framework for thinking through your biases

» A personal code sets a standard for leadership integrity

» A personal code protects your character

The Character-Based, Decision-Making Model from the Josephson Institute of Ethics is insightful: Please visit their website at www. josephsoninstitute.org[1] for a more in-depth understanding of their helpful model. Three principles from this model can help leaders make more ethical decisions:

1. All decisions must take into account and reflect a concern for the interests and well-being of affected individuals. Always help and seek to avoid harm to those touched by your decisions.

2. Ethical values and principles always take precedent over non-ethical ones. Perceiving the difference can be difficult when people feel tension between what they might want or need and ethical principles that might deny their desires.

3. It is ethically proper to violate an ethical principle only when it is clearly necessary to advance another true ethical principle for the greatest balance of good in the long run. When a situation presents competing ethical values and principles, the final decision should create the greatest amount of good and the least amount of harm to the greatest number of people.

The Josephson principles offer a framework for approaching an ethical dilemma. With that perspective in mind, what does a leader of character do when facing the inevitable ethical crossroads in business and in life? Seven questions help me structure my own ethical decision-making process:

Q1 – What are my personal values that inform what is right for me in this situation?

Q2 – What are my biases that might influence how I apply my values to the dilemma?

Q3 – What is the primary issue in this situation? What are the secondary issues?

Q4 – What are the facts from all perspectives?

Q5 – Who are the stakeholders and how will they be helped or harmed by the outcome?

Q6 – What are the options I could consider in the scenarios of how this could be resolved?

Q7 – What outcome will help the most, hurt the least?

Character is tested in the times of ethical turmoil. Your integrity can be affirmed, even by people who may not agree with your final decision, when they know three things: (a) the values that informed your decision, (b) the biases you managed in the decision-making process, (c) the outcome helped the most and hurt the least.

THE CORE

Knowing your values ahead of time will empower you when faced with an ethical situation where the right answer is not clear. Use a structured process to work through a reasoned sequence of steps that will lead to the greatest good and the least harm to the most people. Values and ethical choices are the calling card of integrity for leaders of positive character.

REFLECTION QUESTIONS: If you could rewind and work though an ethical dilemma from an earlier day, what would you do differently? How would it have changed the final decision and outcome?

THE HIDDEN PRICE OF LEADING: THE CALLING AND THE COST

Consider the cost before committing to the cause. The personal price of leadership has a storyline that non-leaders may not fully understand or appreciate. Not everyone will be supportive of the fact that you are the leader, let alone how you are leading. Once committed to the role, you become the target of someone's criticism, challenge, gossip, rumor, or attack. It is not a question of "if" but "when."

THE EMOTIONAL PRICE

CRITICISM. This is the disapproving attitude from team members who assume they know more or think they are a better leader than you.

CHALLENGE. This is the defiant action of the team member who wants your position as leader and will disagree with most of what you do and how you do it.

GOSSIP. This is the somewhat truthful information that is inappropriately shared about you publicly or privately including the teller's spin on the facts.

RUMOR. This is the information someone has conjured up to imply that you may not know what you are doing or that some past attitude, word, or action disqualifies you.

ATTACK. This is the strategy of the accuser, sometimes using humor, who derides your competence and ultimately your character to try to force or embarrass you out of leadership.

A DIVISIVE TEAM MEMBER

They come in all shapes and sizes as do the reasons for their attitudes and actions. Some may not agree with the philosophical premise of your vision, mission, values, and strategy. Some may not fully understand the normal and predictable challenges that are inherent in the current stage of development during this season in the organization's life cycle. They assume that the normal and predictable problems are the result of your incompetent leadership. Others are just jealous that you were selected for the role rather than them. Some bring negative baggage from the rest of their lives. Those issues interrupt their ability to effectively follow as a fully engaged team member.

SUSTAINING LEADERSHIP

A test of leadership is one's ability to emotionally withstand the subtle and sometimes overt hostility toward your leadership. So how do sustaining leaders respond?

BE CONFIDENT IN YOUR CALLING. Leadership is having the certitude to set the strategic course and get your team working collaboratively toward calculated deliverables.

MEET THE OPPONENT. Opposition is like an infectious disease to every other team member. What they do will undermine every effort to align and engage each team member. Confronting is best done in private but not alone.

LISTEN WITH AN OPEN MIND. Criticism and challenge invite the leader to go back to the drawing board for review, reflection, and evaluation of assumptions. Once you complete your due diligence and confirm your direction, then lead boldly even if it means releasing and replacing the critic. The typical mistake is waiting too long to take that action for the sake of the team.

THE CORE

Leadership is never about a legacy of popularity. Leadership is about integrity and character. The effort to appease all critics rarely pays off in getting to the goal in a way that everyone is eager to celebrate. Sustaining leaders are willing and able to pay the price of knowing that not everyone will like them or agree with their pathway to success. Popularity will be expressed at your retirement party because people have observed the consistency of your humility, determination, sacrifice, and results. The consistency of your character will empower you to benefit from but also withstand the critics.

REFLECTION QUESTIONS: Do you want people to recall your accomplishments or recognize and respect your values at your funeral? Do you lead in such a way that people know and respect your values?

CHARACTER MULTIPLIER #2

*Respect: The Interpersonal Side
of Character is What You Think
About Other People*

◆

*If respect is earned, it's transactional.
If respect is given, it's a gift.*

A Civil Workplace: Ten Culture-Climate Questions

At the heart of a civil workplace is the value of respect among all the diverse personalities, workstyles, and job titles represented. *Respect* is not what someone earns from you. If it's earned, then it's transactional and takes time to respect another. Respect is a gift you give to another person regardless of how different they may be in values, background, and ways of doing life. Certainly, people can lose our respect by their attitudes, words, or actions, but we choose to start work relationships by respecting others. It is a down payment in the relationship, and it's an investment in the culture of the organization. It reflects character.

The respect that leaders give to team members contributes to their loyalty, engagement, alignment, and productivity. Qualities of a person who shows *respect* include: affirmation, appreciation, admiration, recognition, and consideration. Qualities of a person who lacks respect include: disregard, contempt, disdain, ignore, marginalize, and neglect. Respect is central in the culture and climate of any organization that values positive character.

> » Culture describes the values-driven ideal of how team members at all employment levels are expected to work together in achieving strategic business outcomes.

> » Climate is the moment-by-moment reality of how consistently every employee lives out those values.

The Culture Gap measures the distance between the ideal and the real. It varies with every leader and every team member for a variety of work or personal reasons. Understanding the dynamics of your culture will help you close the gap. The following *Ten Culture-Climate Questions* will provide a diagnosis on how wide the gap is in your team, department, division, or organization.

TEN CULTURE-CLIMATE QUESTIONS

1. Are the mission, vision, values, and strategy clear and consistently communicated to everyone?

2. How prevalent are political minefields that must be navigated and negotiated to compete for limited resources?

3. What are the spoken or unspoken rules, and does anyone get a pass?

4. Are there personalities who set the positive or negative mood for everyone else?

5. Are there intentional team-building activities that enhance camaraderie and contribute to trust?

6. Is the company a collection of silos, or do teams and team members get to work collaboratively across workplace boundaries?

7. How is conflict perceived and managed?

8. How is failure addressed and success celebrated?

9. Are people micromanaged or given full responsibility and full authority to execute on assignments? In other words, how is authority exerted?

10. How is work-life balance modeled and encouraged?

How wide is the gap between your ideal culture and the daily reality of how consistently each team member lives out the values that define the culture of your team, department, division, or entire organization?

THE CORE

Leaders shape culture (the ideal). Team members determine climate (the real). How big is the gap in your organization? In your department? In your team? In you? As leaders, it is easy to overestimate the narrowness of the gap. Climate is affected by an ineffective leader or a toxic team member. Use the *Ten Culture-Climate Questions* and discuss each one with your executive team. Better yet, use a confidential online survey tool to get a cross-section of responses on these questions from every employment level in your organization. Then strategize how to close the gap that varies by department, leader, team, and team member.

REFLECTION QUESTIONS: Which of the *Ten Culture-Climate Questions* is the most troubling? Which one is most important in your development of greater character and impacting your positive influence?

AN ENVIRONMENT OF KINDNESS: CINDERELLA'S CODE

The Cinderella story was retold once again by Disney in 2015.[1] In the movie, Cinderella vowed to live her life according to a simple code that was expressed in her mother's parting words just before she died. In this magical retelling of a favorite fairytale, leaders and followers can both gain great insights. Sometimes the greatest leadership insights about character come from the most unlikely sources. Let's consider Cinderella's code together.

HAVE COURAGE AND BE KIND

HAVE COURAGE. Leading courageously requires confidence that walks the fine line between arrogance and humility. Courage comes with clarity about the organizational vision, mission, values, and strategy. Courage is the result of a leader's brutal honesty regarding their own leadership capacity and the cluster of competencies needed to execute their role and advance the company's vision. Leadership courage is that ability to "see more than others see...to see further than others see...and to see before others see" to quote Leroy Eimes. And once you SEE IT, courage is the ability to DO IT when others question, criticize, or quit. How courageous of a leader are you?

BE KIND. Kindness is the other side of leading. It represents the soft skills of leadership which focus more on relationships than on results. Kindness is reflected in your attitudes, your words, and your actions. If your attitude is infused with kindness, then your words are more likely to be filled with kind expressions to others. When you think and talk kindly, then your behavior demonstrates that active expression of respect toward those who society tells us are less important.

One area of leadership competency modeling is *interpersonal savvy* which appropriately navigates among various personalities, strengths, and work styles. Emotions are always in play as a built-in warning system when people collide. High EQ is at the core of interpersonal savvy, because we have feelings more quickly than we have rational thoughts. If kindness is a personal value that demonstrates your respect of others who are different, then as a leader of character, you will always allow your thoughts to catch up to your feelings before reacting or responding. Kindness becomes a personal choice that influences attitudes, words, and actions. How kind of a leader are you? Do you feel you have balance in your leadership style?

THE CORE

Character is not that complicated when you narrow the discussion of respect down to two ideas. At the end of every day, ask yourself how you are doing with the fairytale values: Courage and Kindness.

REFLECTION QUESTIONS: When have you led courageously? When have you led with kindness? When was kindness missing in a leadership moment? How will you lead tomorrow in light of what you realized today?

10

HIERARCHICAL ELITISM: WHEN LEADERS DON'T MODEL THE WAY

There is a danger in climbing the corporate ladder. It can change how you see and respond to those still below. When you are just one step above most, your attitude is still appropriate, but when you make it to that special club, you can easily insulate yourself from the rest. Do you think it can't happen to you? Consider the social interactions in the hallway as you pass by looking too busy or focusing on your latest text message. How about the privilege of going to the Executive Dining Room rather than sitting in the cafeteria with everyone else? How about when you sit at the reserved table for more formal organizational events. Your perceived attitude and accompanying actions do major damage in the minds of those who know they will never climb that high in the company.

Merriam-Webster defines pecking order as "the basic pattern of social organization within a flock of poultry in which each bird pecks another lower in the scale without fear of retaliation and submits to pecking by one of higher rank.[1]" Broadly speaking, *Merriam-Webster* describes this as a dominance hierarchy in a group of social animals. It's where we get the phrase, "pecking order," and it plays out in our own social hierarchies. Brian Barth, author of *The Secrets of Chicken Flock's Pecking Order*, said, "Bigger, stronger, and more aggressive chickens bully their way to the top of the flock by pecking the others into submission with their pointy beaks. First, they strut about, fluff their feathers, and squawk, but if that doesn't get the point across, they peck. It can get violent. Sometimes blood is drawn.[2]" Okay, at work we don't draw blood, thankfully, but this is an insightful metaphor for leaders. A pecking order culture can negatively impact the value and practice of respecting differences.

Nine Pecking Order Rules of Grace for Senior Leaders

1. Don't consistently come late and leave early to any meeting because you are too busy with more important things. If the meeting really matters, then fully invest in the process with others in attendance. It means arriving on time. It means not constantly double-booking your calendar.

2. While in the meeting, set all technology aside. A life-shattering emergency rarely happens. Most urgent messages can wait for a reply until your meeting is over. If you are continually distracted by other more important things via your technology, then why did you even attend the meeting? Your actions

model a lack of respect to everyone else in the room. When it's your turn to talk you will probably expect everyone's focused attention.

3. Learn to use your transitional times intentionally. When you walk to another office, another building, the rest room, or to lunch, take time to notice whomever happens to be on that pathway with you. Conversational exchanges can be managed in a few seconds and communicate that you are not too important to smile or ask another person a question about something that matters to them.

4. In all social encounters, ask twice as much as you tell. Be an includer who knows how to interrupt the dominators so you can pull in the quieter introverts who won't fight for equal airtime.

5. Pay attention to the "nobodys." Learn their names and ask them meaningful questions. They are important, after all.

6. Smile, look people in the eye, say "Hello," and call them by name whenever possible.

7. At corporate events assign your leadership team to specific social locations in the room, around the board room table, or at the tables provided in a larger gathering. Spread out to cover the crowd rather than cloister safely together.

8. Avoid the insider information that only the elite are privy to. If you have been together as senior leaders socially, try to keep the details of your gatherings or travels to your private conversations.

9. In simple terms, just be a human being with people at all employment levels. Give those down the pecking order as much time and attention as you reasonably can.

THE CORE

Leadership is as much about the soft skills of positive influence as the hard skills of effective action. The further up the hierarchy, the more you may want to justify the lack of interpersonal savvy because you are rewarded for working on strategy and key outcomes. If you want to develop a pipeline of emerging leaders for the next chapter of your organization, then learn to master the interpersonal competencies that support the journey from the top tier of the organization to the bottom line.

REFLECTION QUESTIONS: Can you identify someone you've been treating as less important than you? People of character work to level the social playing field and flatten any unhealthy hierarchy. Are you working on either?

HOW TO SHUT UP: WHEN LEADERS TALK MORE THAN EVERYONE ELSE

Sustainable leaders invest more effort in learning to ask good questions than striving to tell good answers. Are you an Asker or a Teller? Want to lead for the long haul? Learn the art of query. Then be attentive to what you hear.

WHY DO YOU NEED TO LISTEN MORE?

The Iceberg of Ignorance

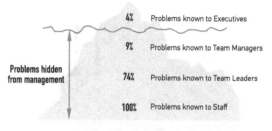

4%   Problems known to Executives

9%   Problems known to Team Managers

74%   Problems known to Team Leaders

100%   Problems known to Staff

Problems hidden from management

© theLDG.org

The Iceberg of Ignorance is a term coined by Sidney Yoshida who studied the work and leadership habits of the Japanese car manufacturer, Calsonic.[1] It is a reminder that the higher you are in leadership the less you really know about the problems below the surface. The only way to know more is to let your asking overtake your telling. The myth of leadership is that we are supposed to know everything. It's a myth. We don't. We can't. That's why you need to build a rhythm of wandering around your organization and ask anyone and everyone: "What do I need to know from you today?" Then stop talking and listen. Yes, you heard me. Shut up is what I'm actually trying to say! You're not used to that, but it will be incredibly valuable.

SEVEN PRACTICES OF GREAT ASKERS

SEQUENCE. Formulate a series of questions in light of your information goals. Write them out to stay on track. Do a second draft to refine them further.

LISTEN. Once you ask the first question, then be attentive without comment or correction.

SILENCE. Practice the disciplined pause. Never interrupt those moments that allow the other person time to reflect before speaking.

DISTINGUISH. Take time to delineate between facts and speculation. You are looking for certitude not personal bias.

ACT. Respond to what you have heard. The next step might be your follow-up question. Know what it is.

SUMMARIZE. Collate the ideas you have heard in your own summary to confirm with the other person that you have understood correctly.

LOOP. Circle back to each person to provide an update of what has happened as a result of what was discussed.

Becoming a great Asker necessitates learning to be an engaged and open-minded listener. Both demonstrate respect in every interpersonal exchange.

THE CORE

Asking and then listening are the best indicators of respect. Asking great questions will not happen without preparation. It's actually hard work to ask thoughtful questions. If you are not a good *Asker*, consider books such as, *Questions That Work* by Andrew Finlayson. Then apply my 24-25-51 Rule of Communication: *Talk* 24% of the time and have something to say that team members need to hear. *Ask* 25% of the time by formulating thought provoking questions. *Listen* 51% of the time. That's over half on purpose! That might be your biggest challenge of leading.

REFLECTION QUESTIONS: Which part of the 24-25-51 Rule of Communication is the hardest for you? Having something to say that team members need to hear? Asking thought provoking questions? Listening for understanding without interrupting? Be a leader who demonstrates character in your respect of others.

RESPECT ◆ 12

BLINDSIDED: THE TOXIC TEAM MEMBER

Critics are a dime a dozen. Freedom of speech allows the critic an opportunity to think, say, and act in ways that communicate their disapproval of you and your leadership. Organizational values define the culture which may monitor the public expressions of the critic, but then their divisiveness can be heard in the private conversations behind closed doors. Once in a while, the critic is bold enough to confront or blind side you unexpectedly. Some are calculating enough to use humor as a commentary of their disapproval and a cover up of their real thoughts. How do leaders respond? How should leaders of respectful character respond? How do you demonstrate respect in the moments when others don't? How are you responding to these situations?

When the Critic Shows Up

If you accept the idea that every leader is criticized, then you can see the power of advanced decision making. It prepares you to expect and be ready for those blindside moments. Understand the difference between constructive criticism and divisive criticism. Then be ready with an appropriate and scripted response that is ready to go.

1. Listen attentively to those who have earned the right to be heard

Others may have critical or even valuable feedback, but they have not taken the time to positively invest in and support the organization's mission, your calling, and your assignment as a leader. Many critics just want you to do it their way rather than your way. Others may be envious that you were selected for the job. And there are always some people who need to be critical in order to be negative. It's how they are wired. They are the self-appointed judge and jury of everyone else. Constructive criticism is based on principle. Divisive criticism is based on personal preference. While divisive criticism may originate from a deeply held principle, it is most often clouded and overrun by personal preference. Tell those who have not earned the right to be heard "thank you" and encourage them to invest that critical energy in doing their job. Then keep leading. Listen but don't dwell on the person or the criticism in ongoing thoughts or conversations.

2. Stop long enough to consider what you should learn from the constructive critic

Delay your defensive response with time given to honestly consider the feedback, especially from those who have earned the right to be heard. Tell them you will think about their ideas and get back to them. Buying time takes the emotion out of blindside moments. Reflection is an insightful filter and can lead to transformational change. Does their idea have validity at this time?

...Can you adapt your leadership approach to the needs that exist in the current season of organizational development?

...What are the obstacles to implementing the idea?

...Do you have the resources to overcome those obstacles?

...What is the return on investment if it is correct?

...What's the risk of failure if it is wrong?

There is value in feedback from those who are committed to the mission, your calling, and your and leadership role. They may only see part of the big picture that you have access to, but they might still have insights worth considering. Senior leaders carry the responsibility for strategy alongside operations. The strategic work of analyzing and synthesizing the relevant data helps you see around the corner of what others might not yet see.

3. DECIDE, SAY "THANK YOU," AND MOVE ON

Once you decide an appropriate response, then loop back to the individual who has addressed principle rather than preference. If you are applying their idea, then thank them as well as give them credit in any public references. If you are not applying their idea, then explain your rationale and encourage their continuing voice in the future. Then move on. Keep leading with confidence but not with arrogance as if you know it all. Leaders of character are collaborative in getting the best ideas on the table from those who support their leadership and believe in the mission. It's your way of demonstrating respect for every team member.

4. MUSINGS ON THE BLINDSIDE MOMENTS

Leadership is all about sustaining positive influence that leads to effective action. Critics enjoy derailing leaders for many different reasons with varying motivations. Anticipate the attitudes, the words, and the actions that go along with this. Some are adept at wrapping their critical spirit in words that appear to be harmless moments of humor. Look past the momentary laughs to consider their motives. They may be reacting out of their own personal baggage more than anything you have said or done. Although it feels personal, it's often not about you at all. Keep leading in spite of them. Eventually everyone catches on to their skewed agenda. These actions can be a career derailer for those whose divisive ways are destructive to the entire team.

THE CORE

Never hesitate to confront the critic and explore their motives,
but understand it is important to do so face to face and in
a private meeting but with an objective third party present.
Divisiveness is infectious, so these are important things to
address. Invite them to get on board. When their attitude,
words, and actions continue, the leadership mistake, admitted
by many, is waiting too long to confront, learn from, reassign,
retrain, or release and replace them.

REFLECTION QUESTIONS: Can you recall the first time you
were blindsided by a critic? How long did you carry the emotion
from that moment? Are you still recalling it? Can you still feel it? It's
time to forgive them, forget it, and move on. Where are you at with
this today? Is it getting easier?

RESPECT ◆ 13

GRATITUDE: WHAT YOU SAY AND HOW YOU SAY IT

Words are powerful, but it's not just what you say. The source of energy in your words is more about *how* you speak and *why* you say what you do. In the United States, we are reminded on one day annually to be people of gratitude. Thanksgiving is a national holiday that provides a reminder and a time to be thankful. What happens on that day is descriptive of leaders of character who model a culture of gratitude to those who serve above you, alongside you, or below you in the pecking order of organizational hierarchy. It's not just what...but how...and why you say, "Thank you." Gratitude reflects the best of your culture.

Saying "Thank You"

WHAT. Be generous with your words. "Thank you" words include: acknowledge, grateful, indebted, appreciation, gratitude, praise, much obliged, thank you very much, thanks a million, thanks from the bottom of my heart, regards, recognition, and tribute.

HOW. Don't default to text or email. The best option is to say *Thank You* personally. The greatest impact occurs when you send a handwritten note to someone's home. Then their entire household gets to be part of celebrating a job well done.

WHY. A well-crafted *Thank You* rather than a half-hearted *Thanks* leaves people encouraged for months. I know because I've experienced it. Gratitude is connected to appreciation that demonstrates respect for others. Ralph Waldo Emerson said it best, "Cultivate the habit of being grateful for every good thing that comes to you, and to give thanks continuously. And because all things have contributed to your advancement, you should include all things in your gratitude."

THE CORE

Developing a culture of gratitude will have a profound impact on your team and the entire company. The assignment includes employees, customers, vendors, and investors. Find regular opportunities to catch people doing something right. Then say, Thank You! Those eight letters express a gratitude that drives commitment, engagement, productivity, retention, and attraction of new talent. They demonstrate respect for others by a leader of interpersonal character.

REFLECTION QUESTION: To whom can you say *Thank You* today? Say it creatively. Say it publicly when appropriate. Say it meaningfully. Put it in writing. Say it today, and don't stop all year long.

VULNERABILITY: WHAT HAPPENS WHEN YOU ASK?

You've heard the idiom, "clearing the air." It's a phrase that has two primary meanings: (1) To remove or replace stale air or unpleasant odor: "Please open the doors and windows to clear the air in here. It is very stuffy." (2) To discuss or otherwise confront an ongoing troubling issue to alleviate tension or confusion: "Can we meet to clear the air from our last team meeting?"

CLEARING THE AIR

Most of us can identify past moments when we created relational tensions as a result of our attitudes, words, nonverbals, or actions. The end of the year can provide a time to "clear the air." The very nature of your year-end review processes provides a motivation and occasion to make things right with those you lead. It's never too late to check back and simply ask if there is any interpersonal *unfinished business* that needs to be addressed in order to move forward in a more positive way. Two scenarios will warrant further attention:

1. YOU WERE WRONG. Admit your mistake, apologize, and ask for forgiveness. We all make mistakes. Model this for every direct report to influence their leadership journey.

2. YOU WERE MISUNDERSTOOD. Start by listening without justifying or explaining away what was said or done. Then tell your side of the story while committing to the effort needed to change perceptions in the future. Your intent may have been noteworthy, but how you were perceived is the reality of how others continue to see you.

A SIMPLE "HOW TO" FOR YOUR "TO DO"

WHO - Ask your team, especially your direct reports.

WHAT - Let them identify any unfinished business...yours or theirs.

WHEN - Determine when before the end of each year.

WHERE - Meet in private on their turf, not your office and not by email.

WHY - To strengthen the culture and climate of your team.

HOW - Courageously and vulnerably.

THE CORE

Leaders of character are humble enough to admit they make
mistakes in attitudes, words, and actions. Pride gets in the
way of humility which gets in the way of character.

REFLECTION QUESTIONS: With whom do you need to meet
first? When? How will you go about checking in with everyone on
your team?

The ancient word for hypocrite pictures the play actor who is one person on stage but another person off stage. A person of character is the same in both.

PART TWO

CORE COMPETENCE

The organization's long-term success is based on a set of differentiated capabilities and its core competency.

—PEARL ZHU
Author and Global Corporate Executive

COMPETENCE MULTIPLIER #1: LEADING PERSONALLY

COMPETENCE MULTIPLIER #2: LEADING INTERPERSONALLY

COMPETENCE MULTIPLIER #3: LEADING ORGANIZATIONALLY

CORE COMPETENCE: THE PATHWAY TO EFFECTIVE ACTION

◆

The most important thing in terms of your circle of competence is not how large the area is, but how well you've defined the perimeter.

—WARREN BUFFETT CEO, Berkshire Hathaway

The Shadow Side of Competence: Peter's Predictive Principle

In 1969, Dr. Laurence J. Peter and Raymond Hull introduced the corporate world to a concept and book by the same name, *The Peter Principle: Why Things Always Go Wrong*.[1] The thesis of their book suggests that people in a hierarchical organization tend to move up the ladder to a level where they are actually incompetent, and that's where they stay without further promotion. Promotion is often based on the performance in one's previous role. Organizations use the *Nine Box Grid* to consider the performance and potential of individuals in any promotion considerations. My version of the *Nine Box Grid* includes a third important dimension: Personal Drive.

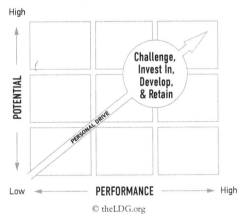

© theLDG.org

Team members who meet expectations in current roles may not demonstrate the personal drive to exceed expectations. As a result, their perceived potential is questioned. The estimate of one's potential gives consideration to their skills and readiness to lead in higher levels of corporate responsibility. Peter and Hull suggest that it's quite common for an individual to reach a level at which they are no longer competent.

One of the toughest transitions is the mid-level leader with operational management responsibilities who is promoted to a more senior leadership position which incorporates responsibility for strategy to improve performance or efficiency. Operational leadership and strategic leadership are two different clusters of competencies in leadership competency models.

The Peter Principle was originally intended to be a satire on organizational development and leadership development. The concept has been given serious consideration as a commentary on the realities and issues of how people are promoted in hierarchical organizational structures. The assumption in the Peter Principle is that even if a person is promoted and competent for that next level of responsibility, they will eventually reach a level where they do not have the skill set and will literally be incompetent. At that point, they are stuck at that new level for the remainder of their career which the authors call "Peter's Plateau."

Scott Adams added insight on this subject in his 1996 book, *The Dilbert Principle: A Cubicle's-Eye View of Bosses*.[2] The idea is similar to the Peter Principle but goes a step further. Adams asserts that organizational hierarchy provides a means to move incompetent people to positions further up in the hierarchy where they are removed from the productivity and important workflow of their company. Adams says that some people in the organization are not very competent in any role, but rather than firing them, they are put into a supervisory role where they have little impact on operations and production.

Competence is key. You either hire for it, train for it, or release because it's lacking. When it's missing, the frequent mistake is waiting too long to retrain, reassign, or release and replace the position with more competent team members. The reality is that people on your team are at varying levels of competence. Training is an option. Mentoring can help. Focused coaching is a transformative investment, but you will never level the playing field where every single employee is a high performer. Typically, whenever you try leveling, you take the whole team down, rarely up. There are emerging leaders with high potential in every organization. You need a system that identifies those contributors who exceed expectations and connect them to a leadership development pipeline to accelerate their natural ability to reach new heights of leading in areas of greater organizational complexity. Three questions help address three different levels of competence:

» EXPECTATION "EXCEEDERS" – What do you say and do to continue to engage, develop, and retain this group as you equip them to manage or lead at higher levels of organizational responsibility?

» EXPECTATION "MEETERS" – What do you say and do to acknowledge that they meet expectations rather than unfairly compare them to the Exceeders? Yet how can you stretch them in new ways to maximize their consistency and value to the team and organization.

» EXPECTATION "MISSERS" – What do you do to challenge this group when identifying benchmark expectations that must be met for them to retain their role? Is it an issue of experience, training, or a lack of personal drive? How long do you carry them before their underperformance affects team productivity and morale? When you don't address the Expectation "Missers," that is when you level the team down and not up!

THE ORGANIZATIONAL ROI: THE CASE FOR COMPETENCE-BASED LEADERSHIP

There is a growing body of research and literature regarding the value of developing leaders at all levels in any organization. This work is meeting a need that leads to an investment of significant resources in developing comprehensive leadership institute programs within companies. Eventually someone on the executive team will ask, "What are we getting for all this money we are spending?" There are key insights in answering that question from the continuing work and research by several organizations including: The Center for Creative Leadership, The Association for Talent Development, Korn Ferry, Bersin by Deloitte, The Conference Board, Development Dimensions International, and the ROI Institute. A White Paper from the Center for Creative Leadership documents the value of the investment in organizations that address leadership development: "Driving Performance: How Leadership Development Powers Success."[3] Not only does leadership development deepen the bench of a leadership team, but four specific things happen when companies invest in the development of emerging leaders:

1. IMPROVE FINANCIAL PERFORMANCE. Leadership development leads to reduced costs, new lines of revenue, and improved customer satisfaction.

2. ATTRACT AND RETAIN TALENT. Leadership development boosts employee engagement, increases the organization's ability to deal with gaps in the talent pipeline, and reduces challenges and costs associated with turnover.

3. DRIVE STRATEGY EXECUTION. Leadership development aligns with business strategy and equips employees with the skills needed to execute and achieve goals.

4. INCREASE SUCCESS IN NAVIGATING CHANGE.
Leadership development increases people's ability to respond quickly in unpredictable business environments. Agility is enhanced.

Kevin Sheridan's blog from the Association for Talent Development, *The Business Case for Leadership Development and Learning*, refers to one study in this growing collection of research.[4] In this joint study, The Conference Board and DDI, a global leadership consulting firm, found the following changes in organizations investing in leadership development training:

» 114% higher sales

» 71% higher customer service

» 42% better operational efficiency

» 48% more product and work quality

» 300 % additional business referrals

» 233% extra cross-selling

» 36% higher productivity

» 90% lower absenteeism

» 49% reduced overtime work (and overtime pay)

» 105% fewer grievances

» 90% less rework

» 60% fewer workplace accidents

» 77% lower turnover

We know enough today to credibly state that developing leaders pays off in contributing to strategic business outcomes as well as the health of organizational culture. In order to operationalize the case for competency-based leadership, I believe the following ingredients are essential:

ORGANIZATIONAL VALUE – The most senior leader(s) must value a developmental culture.

ORGANIZATIONAL COMMITMENT – The value leads to a commitment of organizational resources.

STRUCTURE – Recognizing the need to develop leaders at every level is essential.

POINT PERSON – Identify someone to own the competency development structure and framework.

RECRUITMENT PLAN – This is a pathway that creates the system for participation and completion.

CURRICULUM – Build or buy curriculum using all content delivery systems that achieve intended results.

CELEBRATION – Benchmark achievement in the commitment to inspire and reward lifelong learning.

Competence is half of the formula that contributes to leadership capacity. One's competence represents the skills needed for effective action in their role to accomplish strategic results that benefit the bottom line. Character is the other half of the formula focusing on positive influence in all stakeholder relationships. Attending to competence without attention to character is unsustainable in the long run. When people respect what you accomplish but don't like who you are, it's the formula for disaster that leads to a dissatisfied, disengaged, and occasional toxic workforce. So how does one develop a commitment to competence that leads to effective action?

Three competence multipliers provide a guide for the sustainable leader: Leading Personally (Chapters 15-19), Leading Interpersonally (Chapters 20-24), and Leading Organizationally (Chapters 25-28).

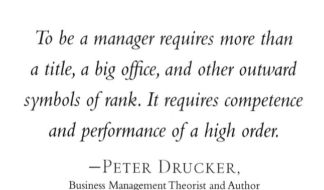

*To be a manager requires more than
a title, a big office, and other outward
symbols of rank. It requires competence
and performance of a high order.*

—PETER DRUCKER,
Business Management Theorist and Author

COMPETENCE MULTIPLIER #1

Leading Personally:
The Foundation of Competence

- ◆ -

To know your own limitations is the
hallmark of competence.

—DOROTHY L. SAYERS
English Writer and Poet

How to Lead in One Word: It's a Gift

The literature of ancient Israel invites any leader to consider the following: *If you have the gift of leadership, then lead with diligence.* Leadership is a gift. It is a gift you are given, and it is a gift you give. So, what is diligence all about? When is the last time you did a personal assessment of your opportunity to lead, your competence to lead, and any gaps that interfere with the outcomes of your leadership? Today might be your day to honestly assess the *Diligence Quotient* in your work of leading.

THE GIFT OF LEADERSHIP

THE GIFT YOU ARE GIVEN - An organization gives you a gift when you are invited to a role of leading others. The gift is given to you when your exceptional performance is continually noticed. It's a risk based on the assumption that you also have the potential to lead in new ways with greater responsibility. Do you know your competency gaps? In other words, are there areas of responsibility in the new role where your "good" competency needs to become a "great" competency? How will you close the gap?

THE GIFT YOU GIVE - Every individual you lead creates the responsibility to invest in their career development. You can offer the gift of feedback, training, delegation of responsibilities, stretch assignments, and promotions. The leadership calling is to be fair with each individual in light of their capacity and readiness. The *Stay Interview* can be an important part of your one-on-one with each team member. Discussing their career plans and the resources for their development communicates your commitment to their aspirations and potential even if they move to a different team or role to make a greater contribution to the organization. Your support of their development leads to a greater chance of retention. Organizations known for development also strengthen their attraction to the best talent in your industry.

THE SINGULAR WORD IS DILIGENCE - It represents your drive to keep learning in order to develop your leadership competence. It is defined as "careful and persistent work or effort." It implies careful attention with haste and speed in doing something that you highly value, aspire to, and love. It is the opposite of waiting to fulfill your leadership responsibility whenever there is time left over at the end of your To Do list each day. Diligent leaders never find time, they make time. Diligence is:

» PASSION. The desire to lead more effectively and efficiently.

» EXPERIENCE. The willingness to take on stretch assignments to enhance your leadership capacity.

» INTENTIONALITY. Delegation to develop high-potential team members to increase overall productivity.

» RETURN ON INVESTMENT. The impact of developing the next generation of leaders.

THE CORE

Is leadership just one of the many things you do, or is it everything you are and do? What is the *Diligence Quotient* in your leadership? What will you do this week to demonstrate the careful attention and persistent work of leading others?

REFLECTION QUESTIONS: How diligent are you? On a 1 to 10 scale (10 is high) how would you rate yourself in the areas of: Passion, Experience, Intentionality, and ROI? How would you rate your overall success in developing the next generation of leaders?

16

LEADERS SEE
AROUND THE
CORNER:
WHAT'S NEXT?

Leaders learn to look around the corner to see what others do not yet see. They think in reverse from deliverable outcomes to present realities. They think backward in order to move forward. An effective strategy considers three calculated maneuvers: (1) Assessment (2) Preferred Future and (3) The Sequence of Change. Implement these ideas and you are on your way to becoming a strategic leader.

Assessing Your Organization's Current Realities

Assignment #1

Review the data. What story does the data tell about the shortcomings of your current reality? What are your organization's strengths, weaknesses, opportunities, and threats (SWOT)?

COMPETENCIES NEEDED. *Analysis* to understand what the data says, *Synthesis* to understand what the data means, and *Communication* to describe your current state honestly, concisely, and with clarity.

ACTION STEPS. Do an honest assessment of where the organization is today. The conclusion will range on a continuum of emotions from elation to disappointment to frustration. Review each aspect of the organization's storyline until you understand where the story leaves off and where you are picking it up.

1. COLLECT - Find out all the versions of your story: employees, customers, vendors, investors, and even your competition. Consider the following evaluative questions: What do they think you are good at...bad at? How does their perception compare to the reality in your own estimation? Are you a thought leader with any best practices you can contribute to the industry at large? Why are you losing out to the competition? What should you keep doing, change or update, stop doing, or start doing? What distinguishes you from everyone else?

2. ORGANIZE - Identify the categories of feedback and simply sort the information. Whatever your categories, separate the positive, negative, and neutral ideas.

3. ANALYZE - Spend time objectively reviewing each category. Analysis implies that you take something apart to study it. You want to understand every piece of the story and the themes emerging within the data. Keep an open mind.

4. SYNTHESIZE - Begin to make connections so you know the reality of where your organization is today. What is your current state? How did you get here? What are your strengths, challenges, and opportunities? Opportunity is all about finding the favorable winds that are blowing toward your preferred or necessary destination.

5. SYNOPSIS - Summarize the story to provide an overview of where you have been, where you are today, and the beginning of what's next.

ARTICULATE A PREFERRED FUTURE

Assignment #2

Announce a preferred future. In the analysis, you gain clarity on where you are today and where you need to be tomorrow. It's the leadership perspective of seeing around the corner what others do not yet see. What is the ultimate outcome of fulfilling your daily mission while living the values of your organizational culture? What adjustments will be needed in your strategy, structure, and staffing to respond to the changing market, competition, and technology?

COMPETENCE NEEDED. *Managing the vision.* Leaders optimistically look to future possibilities. They create a compelling vision, verbalize it, personally own it, motivate others to buy in, and align organizational resources to achieve it.

ACTION STEPS. If assessment begins to clarify "what" your storyline is, then changing to achieve a preferred future state begs for an understanding of "why." If you are not content with the current realities and have a sense of where you need to go, then explaining why the change is needed becomes important to successfully navigate the chaos of change.

1. PICTURE - Since pictures are worth a thousand words, craft an inspiring visual of what the organization will look like when you arrive. What is the next destination in your organizational journey? What will it be like to be part of that organization compared to what it is like today?

2. WHY - What realities about today prevent you from settling in and just staying the course? Share the specifics of the current trend line if changes are not made. What will the organization look like in one year or five years if the trajectory is not altered? What opportunities are being missed if you are not proactive in writing the next pages of your company's history?

3. ASSUMPTIONS - Realistically share the assumptions that guide, support, and define the direction you are headed. This is the hard data that creates the framework around the picture you have created for a new tomorrow. Assumptions include an honest appraisal of what the change adventure implies. The realities of sacrifice, loss, and pain are more effectively communicated by the storyteller than interpreted by the reader.

THE SEQUENCE OF CHANGE

Assignment #3

Close the gap. Think in reverse order from your preferred future back to your current reality. What steps will be needed to move from here to there and close the gap that exists?

COMPETENCIES NEEDED. (1) *Strategy* is the leader's orientation in accurately anticipating market trends while identifying the steps needed to get to the goal. Strategy includes the uncertainty of endless variables, understanding risk assumptions, and projecting scenarios of how things can work together. (2) *Change Management* is the ability to explain the What, the How, and especially the Why of anticipated changes. Change leaders understand the varying timelines of adopting to change, including the need to manage the transitions that result from the actual moment of change.

ACTION STEPS. Strategy is knowing when it is time for an organization to move on to a new future state. Strategic leadership involves knowing how to get from today's reality to tomorrow's possibility.

1. OBSTACLES - Unravel the complexities of what it means to make that move. The more your teams understand that you are fully aware of the challenges, the more they are willing to follow you through the transition. Be specific. Be thorough. Be realistic. Be optimistic. Be humble. Be empathetic.

2. SCENARIOS - Articulate the options that are available. The various avenues you might consider will satisfy different criteria. Describe each alternative and listen to your front-line teams to articulate the pros and cons of each. None will be perfect. Try to find the perfect answer and you will

frustrate everyone. Compare each scenario according to effort and impact, connection to each stakeholder group, ultimate alignment to your vision, mission, and values, and a realistic timeline required to reach the destination.

3. RESOURCES – Once the options are on the table, let the specifics of the resources required for each one help narrow your list. What people, facilities, capital, IT, structures, and systems will it take to execute each scenario? Strategic leadership is always about managing limited resources according to the right priorities.

4. CHANGE – What is the depth and breadth of change required by your best-case scenario? What level of resistance is expected? Strategic leadership requires the ability to positively influence individuals and teams to make connections across organizational boundaries and align resources for efficiency and effectiveness.

THE CORE

Don't forget: Strategy is the noun. Strategic is the adjective.
Strategic leadership never moves forward with 100% certainty
as to the destination or the route to get there. Your leadership
calling is to see what others do not yet see. The collaborative
invitation is to find the best way to get there. Strategic Leaders
determine the pathway with their teams fully engaged in the
considerations, discussions, and final decisions, while never
feeling afraid to be the voice that initiates, clarifies, and leads
to consensus, or to leader-initiated conclusions.

REFLECTION QUESTIONS: Who could lead each of three work teams: Assessment, Future State, and Change? Participation creates early ownership and buy-in. Do you conclude that this work needs to be ongoing with a formal annual check-in with your executive team to answer the basic questions: Where are we? Where are we going?

17

LEADERS INITIATE CONTINUAL CHANGE: UNAVOIDABLE REALITIES

Technological advancements, new markets, smart competitors, and strategic planning all lead to the same outcome: *change*. It's inevitable in organizations that choose to step out into an informed unknown. Continual improvement implies incremental steps to move from the current state to a preferred future state. Change is both uncomfortable and your forever friend.

Ten Unavoidable Realities About Change

#1 - It's always there. Change is not going away anytime soon.

#2 - Most don't like it.

#3 - People adapt on differing timelines.

#4 - Some resist it as long as possible.

#5 — Many mistakenly assume the work is over at the moment of change.

#6 - Those who get on board early are not usually your best advocates.

#7 - What motivates people is understanding why rather than knowing what or how.

#8 - It's messy and rarely goes as planned.

#9 - Adjustments are always needed.

#10 - In the short run, it looks like a mistake. The long view will tell the full story.

Change leadership necessitates change management. Change needs to be managed up to the moment of the change event, and more so after the transition begins. Leaders strategize *what* needs to change in moving from the current state to a preferred future state. Then leaders articulate *why*. Front-line team members are the best resource for *how* to make it happen. Leaders also understand the *why* gets fuzzy every thirty days or so. Find the stories that illustrate early successes. Let the story makers be the story tellers.

REFLECTION QUESTIONS: Is every employee part of your process improvement initiative? What is your means of collecting ideas from all levels of employment? Are people expected to suggest improvement ideas for greater efficiency and productivity? Who leads the review and consideration of the ideas suggested? Do you report out to your organization on changes that result from ideas they suggested? Do you acknowledge whomever suggested an idea or do you acknowledge the idea but keep the person anonymous?

18

LEADERSHIP AGILITY: IN TIMES OF TRANSITION

The tendency in the early days of anyone's leadership is to oversimplify an understanding of the profound complexity of leading. It is a one-size-fits-all misunderstanding. The misinformed leader says, "This is who I am and how I lead." In fact, those who choose to lead are called to be agile in adjusting leadership styles to meet both organizational challenges and opportunities.

THREE LEADERSHIP QUESTIONS

What are we doing, how are we doing it, and why are we doing it?

ANSWERING THE "WHAT" QUESTION: IT IS THE CORE OF STRATEGIC THINKING. Every team member needs clarity in knowing what business you are in. Confusion or misunderstanding by any team member interferes with high performance in the team's achievement of strategic business outcomes. In your current season of organizational development, leaders sharpen their communication efforts and speak directly to the organization's reason for being.

ANSWERING THE "HOW" QUESTION: IT IS THE CORE OF FOSTERING CULTURE. Values shape the ideal picture of organizational culture and climate in describing how people work together even with vendors or customers to effectively reach shared goals. In this season of organizational development, leaders commit to model the behaviors demonstrating organizational values. In addition, they expect it from everyone else by calling for consistent accountability and giving immediate feedback to those who miss these expectations.

ANSWERING THE "WHY" QUESTION: IT IS THE CORE OF VISION CASTING. Answering *What* and *How* should be standard objectives in any organization. Answering the Why question is the differentiator that creates focus and alignment and leads to increased engagement and loyalty. Leaders effectively answering the *Why* question work hard to capture the stories that illustrate the difference made by what the organization does. This quality of leadership illustrates the mission and values of our best corporate leaders. These agile leaders take time to notice, to remember, to ask, to tell, and to retell the best practice accounts of what it means to be connected to this company.

YOUR AGILITY AS A LEADER

Each of these organizational movements requires a different emphasis in leading. It is not an either/or choice but rather a both/ and opportunity. Personal leadership intelligence is knowing the competency mix required at the intersection where each of these three movements meet.

REMINDER #1 - The organization does not adjust to fit the leader. Leaders adapt to use the right mix of competencies to meet the needs that emerge during any stage of organizational development.

REMINDER #2 - Organizations are either developing, stabilized, or deteriorating. Leaders address the competency gaps needed for the normal and predictable challenges in the current stage of organizational development in order to move into the next stage of organizational maturity.

THE CORE

Are you willing to adjust your leadership competency profile to more effectively and efficiently meet the challenges of where your company will be if you get to that preferred future?

REFLECTION QUESTIONS: Which area of your leadership needs your immediate attention: What, How, or Why? How often do you revisit the "why" to remind every team member that what they do is important?

19

YOUR PERSONAL COMMUNICATION AUDIT: SIX REFLECTIVE QUESTIONS

Times of change, crisis, or uncertainty leverage the most significant leadership competency: communication. The best leaders will scramble to make sense of what's happening and articulate a way through. The best advice is to communicate frequently and empathetically with vulnerable transparency. Leaders always benefit by taking the time to review and reflect on their leadership communication before, during, and after the change, crisis, or uncertainty. It requires learning from what's happening to be prepared for what's coming next.

How Effective Is Your Leadership Communication?

Marshall Goldsmith introduced me to a twenty-one-day reflection exercise. He has given me permission to use it in my executive coaching work and in this book. An example of the Daily Reflection Exercise is included in the Afterword at the end of the book. Here it is applied to the important topic of communication. Review the six questions that connect to the most common aspects of leadership communication. Use the simple 1-5 Likert Scale to evaluate yourself at the end of each day for 21 workdays.

1 = you blew it and 5 = you hit a home run

VERBAL. Did I do my best to carefully choose my words and mindfully consider how those words were expressed?

NON-VERBAL. Did I do my best to ensure that my body language credibly reflected what I wanted to communicate?

LISTENING. Did I do my best to genuinely listen for understanding rather than agreement?

WRITTEN. Did I do my best to craft my written words in texts, emails, letters, and other documents and consider how they would be interpreted?

FEEDBACK. Did I do my best to appropriately provide positive feedback publicly and negative feedback privately?

CONFLICT. Did I do my best today to ensure that any current conflict was focused on ideas, not individuals?

Want to honestly know how good of a communicator you are? Identify your blind spots...things you don't know about yourself, but those closest to you do. The only way to uncover your blind spots is to ask for feedback. Ask the people you live with, then ask the people you work with. Ask anyone you interact with often. Ask your everyday staff, direct reports, peers, senior leaders, and even the UPS driver. Consider the feedback valuable, and use it to own your blind spots and work on specific ways to become a better communicator.

. . . . ☕ . . . .

THE CORE

Communication is the primary competence of a leader. Just because something was said does not mean it was heard, understood, or agreed with. As you get to know your team and key stakeholders, the development of this core competence implies that you adapt your communication strategy to the uniqueness of each listener or group of listeners.

REFLECTION QUESTIONS: Which of the six aspects of communication is your greatest strength compared to the other five? Which one do you stumble over most often? What will you do to enhance these tools in your leadership toolbox?

COMPETENCE MULTIPLIER #2

Leading Interpersonally:
The Relational Side of Competence

.... ◆ ....

Either I'm seeing others straightforwardly as
they are - as people like me who have needs and
desires as legitimate as my own - or I'm not...
One way, I experience myself as a person among
people. The other way, I experience myself as
the person among objects.

LEADERSHIP AND SELF-DECEPTION
The Arbinger Institute

20

HIRING THE BEST: THREE INTERVIEW QUESTIONS

Hiring mistakes negatively impact two primary organizational resources: time and money. The corporate best practices are a reminder that you either invest time on the front end or on the back end. Hire hard and manage easy unless you'd rather hire easy and manage hard. There are things you can do to improve your hiring practices. Three questions will help determine your choice to make an offer or to keep looking.

YOUR THREE FINAL HIRING DECISION QUESTIONS

Q1 - The Competency Question.

Can they do the job? Are there gaps in the skills needed to meet expectations? Can you afford the time to get them up to speed? What assessments are you using to determine gaps and work readiness?

Q2 - The Motivation Question

Will they do the job? Performance and potential are two dimensions of the Nine Box Grid. What's missing in this insightful matrix is the aspect of personal drive. Past performance is no guarantee nor is perceived potential. How motivated are they...and why?

Q3 - The Culture Question

Will you like them while they do the job? In part, organizational culture is shaped by stated values and accountability for the behavioral expectations connected to each value. The outlier personality is often a management nightmare and potentially toxic to the team. Involve a cross-section of your company in the interview process. Consider the intuitive insights people have about a candidate's cultural fit.

THE CORE

Hiring the best is very hard work. Today's employment opportunities create a challenge in attracting and retaining the best employees. Know when you need to wait and keep looking.

REFLECTION QUESTIONS: In considering the three hiring questions, who on your team would you not hire today? Why? Which of the three hiring decision questions is the most important? What percentage of hires do you prefer to be internal rather than external? What can you learn from past hiring decisions?

BUILDING A
LEADERSHIP
DEVELOPMENT
CULTURE: THE
ABCs

A comprehensive perspective of your company will give an honest assessment of what is needed to develop emerging leaders. Review the six interrogatives to determine how intentional you are in shaping organizational culture to stretch leadership capacity. Do you have a sustainable structure with the systems needed to move emerging leaders from a talent pool into a leadership development pipeline?

WHO? Leadership capacity is defined as the ability to lead effectively in your current role as well as in more complex roles. Have you determined which employment categories are eligible to participate in leadership development initiatives? Once you are clear on this, then how are the individuals identified to move into a leadership pipeline that targets the needs of each level of the organization?

WHAT? Leadership roles vary by the complexity of the assignment and the number of people who report directly or indirectly to that individual. What competencies are in focus in the leadership development training agenda at each level within the organization? This is an important question because leading other leaders requires a different set of competencies than leading managers or managing non-leaders.

WHEN? What is the rhythm of your training components? Does the organization and each team leader understand that the development of team members requires time to complete training modules, participate in coaching, and take on new challenging job assignments that go beyond their current role? Even though individual development requires an investment of time by the team member, that time always has an organizational payoff.

WHERE? The 70-20-10 Rule from the Center for Creative Leadership provides an understanding that most of the developmental impact (70 percent) happens on the job not through new work or more work, but applying new leadership habits in the work you are already doing.

WHY? Leadership development is an investment in people the organization already knows and people who also already know the organization. This builds on an individual's commitment to organizational vision, mission, values, strategy, and existing senior leaders. A development culture is what drives the retention of your high-potential team members as well as attracting the industry's best and brightest.

HOW? Organizational access to leadership development for all emerging leaders includes large group events to provide a clear understanding of leadership as the balance between *positive influence* and *effective action*. The balance depends on the situation, the team, and/or the team member. Once team members move more formally into a leadership pipeline, then you can build on the 70-20-10 framework. Micro learning focused on a leadership competency profile should account for 10 percent of how time is invested in professional development. Coaching on how learning applies should be 20 percent and will identify application scenarios. Remember, 70 percent represents on-the-job stretch assignments that develop new habitual leadership skills.

AN ORGANIZATIONAL EFFECTIVENESS DIAGNOSIS TO ACCELERATE LEADERSHIP DEVELOPMENT

Do you have a system to identify, attract, develop, deploy, and retain the leadership talent your company needs today and into the future?

> » OUTCOMES. Are you satisfied with the outcomes from your existing leadership development process? How are you measuring effectiveness?

> » ALIGNMENT. Is your leadership development initiative intentionally aligned with strategic business outcomes and the

cultural values of the organization? Does your plan enable you to create a profile of core leadership competencies needed by every single leader?

» ONBOARDING. Are you able to achieve those strategic outcomes if a key leader retires or leaves your organization? Have you considered the time and cost to replace and onboard that leader?

» PIPELINE. Do you have a talent pool and leadership pipeline to quickly fill an available leadership role internally?

» SUCCESSION. Do you have a succession model and plan for all levels of key leadership roles?

» ROI. Have you considered the return on investment of an accelerated leadership development program in terms of talent attraction, employee engagement, strategic productivity, and talent retention?

THE CORE

Review each of these interrogatives with your senior leadership to honestly determine your organizational realities, both positive and negative. Decide what you need to change, keep, or add to your process.

REFLECTION QUESTIONS: How ready is your company to identify potential internal candidates for succession planning? Which of the six interrogative questions is yet unanswered? Is your leadership development process lacking? What is one thing you can do to move toward creating a sustainable plan?

THE LEADER-
COACH: INVEST
IN EMERGING
LEADERS

What's the return on investment when developing leaders at every level in any organization? An intentional leadership development process will result in a culture of collaborative leaders whose aligned effort results in best practice innovation, improved operational efficiency, enhanced productivity, and a sustainable pipeline of leaders equipped for organizational expansion and succession planning. The Center for Creative Leadership speaks to this subject in an August 2020 article titled, "4 Reasons to Invest in Leadership Development."[1] In this article, they show that a combination of organizational value and organizational investment in leadership development leads to:

1. Improving bottom-line financial performance

2. Attracting and retaining industry's best talent

3. Driving a performance culture

4. Increasing organizational agility[2]

VALUING AND INVESTING IN DEVELOPMENT

Assume your company does value and does invest in the development of high-potential team members at every employment level. If you used the grid below and randomly asked employees which quadrant describes your culture, what might you learn? Your choices lead to one of four outcomes:

THE ORGANIZATIONAL VALUE AND INVESTMENT GRID

© theLDG.org

How do you operationalize a high value and a high investment in emerging leaders? Search Institute, www.search-institute. org, has been doing social analysis for decades to achieve their rallying cry: *Healthy Communities Healthy Youth*.[2] Their team of social researchers took the counterintuitive route to improve communities, specifically the youth in those cities. They did not do it by addressing the problems that exist but rather the qualities of a healthy community that are missing. Their research identified forty developmental assets of healthy communities. Their strategy includes an assessment to identify which assets are missing in the community. Then they work with the city, schools, faith networks, and business sector to build those missing assets into community life. Organizations can learn from these insights to transform the culture and climate of the workplace and engage team members in achieving shared strategic outcomes for *Healthy Organizations Healthy Employees.*

DEVELOPMENTAL RELATIONSHIPS

One of the core assets for Search Institute is *developmental relationships with important people in their lives.* They define this as, "... close connections through which young people discover who they are, cultivate abilities to shape their own lives, and learn how to engage with and contribute to the world around them." Search Institute has identified five elements of developmental relationships that include twenty actions. What if we applied their research to organizations? Might this help organizational leaders transform dysfunctional cultures and climates in teams, departments, divisions, and entire organizations? Here is a framework based on the Search Institute model for such a scenario including five elements and twenty actions for developmental relationships:

#1 EXPRESS CARE - Show me that I matter to you.

ACTIONS: Be dependable, listen, believe in me, be warm, and encourage.

#2 CHALLENGE GROWTH – Push me to keep getting better.

ACTIONS: Expect my best, stretch me, hold me accountable, and reflect on my failures.

#3 PROVIDE SUPPORT – Help me complete tasks and achieve goals.

ACTIONS: Navigate, empower, advocate, and set boundaries.

#4 SHARE POWER – Treat me with respect and give me a say.

ACTIONS: Respect me, include me, collaborate, and let me lead.

#5 EXPAND POSSIBILITIES – Connect me with people and places that broaden my world.

ACTIONS: Inspire, broaden my horizons, and connect.

THE CORE

Organizations that value and invest in leadership development at every level extend the invitation to each leader to come alongside team members and be the advocate in their development. Whatever you model for them, they are more likely to model the same with those they manage. Whatever you neglect in your busyness, anticipate that they may also neglect when they are busy. The commitment to leading as coach cascades from the top to the bottom of your organization.

REFLECTION QUESTIONS: Which of the five Search Institute categories is most often neglected by you? Within that category, which actions will you begin to model with your direct reports to practice your value and your investment in developing your team?

23

OVER AND UNDER STYLES OF MANAGING: KNOW YOUR TEAM

Steve Jobs famous quote reflects the tension in how we manage and lead people: *It doesn't make sense to hire smart people and tell them what to do; we hire smart people so they can tell us what to do.* The essential ingredient in leading competently is to "hire hard so you can manage easy." Jim Collins, author of *Good to Great*, uses the metaphor of the bus: we need to get those smart people in the right seat on the bus. The right bus and the right seat for everyone still requires competent managers and leaders to align all their resources toward strategic outcomes. The wisdom of leadership is finding the right balance between each team member's competence and assignment. Leaders are always calculating how much management is too much and how much is not enough for each direct report in every role they fulfill. You end up realizing the need to manage each direct report uniquely and not with a one-size-fits-all approach.

OVER MANAGE. The micromanager doesn't empower team members, in large part, because they don't trust them. As a result, direct reports don't get developed, and the organization doesn't get all the value from each team member. The leader doesn't delegate which occupies more of their time in tactical operations with little time or energy left for strategy. They might be subject-matter experts, perfectionists, impatient for results, or just have a need or habit to touch every discussion and every decision. As a result, they lose. Team members lose. The company loses.

UNDER MANAGE. The other competence mistake for leaders is to under manage direct reports. They do need you to supervise their work at an appropriate level. If leaders are not available when help is needed, it may indicate they are too busy with their own To Do list. Some may be afraid to admit they don't have all the answers, or they want to avoid more conflict with a difficult team member. The questions for each team member include: (1) How much of a load are they carrying? (2) How much of your help do they need?

IT'S A BALANCING ACT

A leadership quote that raises the tension in motivating team members says: "A pat on the back is only a few vertebrae removed from a kick in the pants but is miles ahead in results." Ella Wheeler Wilcox was an American author and poet who lived from 1850 to 1918. Where is the leadership fulcrum set point between a pat on the back and a kick in the pants? The People-Task graph illustrates

what Ella Wheeler Wilcox pointed out 100 years ago. The tension for
leaders still exists decades later.

THE PEOPLE - TASK GRAPH

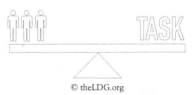

© theLDG.org

TIMES AND TEAM MEMBERS

Leadership is not the time you have left over at the end of your To
Do list. Managing and leading your team and each team member
is everything you do. It must be #1 on your list at the beginning
of every workday, and if there is time left over, then pull out the
rest of your To Do list. Always be asking, "What is needed by each
team member to be successful today?" Success is defined in terms
of effectiveness and efficiency in completing project assignments
with the resources currently available. In every conversation you are
managing the *set point* on the continuum between your task focus
and your people focus. It varies for every team member every day.
Creating systems that self-manage and finding ways to measure the
work within those systems is the pathway from extrinsic motivation
to intrinsic motivation.

Four aspects of competently managing others will help guide leaders
in finding the right balance between over and under…between task
and people.

1. UNDERSTAND BANDWIDTH. Each team member will
   vary in their capability regarding the quantity and quality of
   work they can complete. What can they realistically handle?
   The differences within your team may vary because of training,
   experience, or the drive of the individual. If they exceed

expectations, they are one of your high potentials who may be ready for new stretch assignments as you determine what you can offload in order to take on more strategic tasks. If they meet expectations, that's what they are paid for. If they continually miss expectations, then the choice is to retrain, reassign, or release and replace.

2. COMMUNICATE WITH CLARITY. Eliminate any confusion by providing a clear understanding of what is in scope and out of scope, what success looks like, what resources are available, what level of authority is given to those taking on the responsibility, and who will be responsible for checking in on identified benchmarks. If you are not sure if they "got it," then have them articulate their understanding of what you are asking them to do.

3. DELEGATE DEVELOPMENTALLY. Handing off the responsibility and relinquishing the authority to execute are the two delegation steps. Until you let go, you have not fully delegated the assignment. Invest with a long-term view of getting someone up to speed to effectively take over the task. When you do, it contributes to their development in a stretch assignment and buys you time to devote to the strategy role of leading in order to achieve the productive potential of your team.

4. DESIGN A FORMAL FEEDBACK SYSTEM. Establish how you will formally and informally stay in touch. A weekly summary from each direct report can be completed verbally or in writing. Either approach has strengths and weaknesses. A written summary creates another form to fill out, but it provides a tracking record for future reference. A verbal summary can be done one-on-one or in a team huddle either virtually or in person. The huddle report-out leverages group dynamics and competitive social accountability among that

group of peers. The intent in what I am proposing is to be unusually short and to the point. Four questions suffice:

Q#1 – What did you accomplish this week?

Q#2 – What challenges or obstacles did you run into?

Q#3 – What will you achieve next week?

Q#4 – In what way, if any, can I be of help to you?

THE INFORMAL APPROACH TO ACCOUNTABILITY

Questions are the most powerful tool in your leadership resources. It's not always having the right thing to say. Sometimes your best leadership action is asking the right question. Then be even smarter by listening. Yes, deal with the awkward pause and let the team member have the silent moment to gather their thoughts. Don't rescue the unnerving quietness. How about a few prompts that will intentionally structure those every day and informal conversations in the hallway or on a virtual call? Add to my list in creating your own questions that are part of your approach to holding team members accountable and discovering when they might need your help.

THE OBVIOUS QUESTION: Do you need my help?

THE INQUISITIVE QUESTION: What do I need to know from you today?

THE AWKWARD QUESTION: How are you keeping me from being blindsided in your work on this project?

THE BENCHMARK QUESTION: What's your plan to keep me informed at key decision points in the completion of this project?

THE MISTAKE QUESTION: What are the insights you have gained from the mistake made that will strengthen your work going forward?

THE DEVELOPMENT QUESTION: What skills or resources were needed to complete this project that we did not realize at the beginning?

THE COMPLETION QUESTION: How can I best recognize your accomplishment to celebrate a job well done?

THE VULNERABILITY QUESTION: Am I overmanaging you, or am I undermanaging you?

THE STRETCH QUESTION: Are you ready for a new stretch assignment to develop new skills and equip you to lead at higher levels of organizational complexity?

THE CORE

The leader as coach will take time to discover the capability of each team member. Managing people as part of your leadership is a delicate balance between two extremes: overmanaging or undermanaging. Each direct report needs a different compromise between the two extremes. Know your people. Know when to step in. Know when to back away. Know when to let them fail. Know how to help them learn from the failure as part of their development. The goal is leveraging micro learning with macro application to achieve incremental development.

REFLECTION QUESTIONS: Do you know your team well enough to know who needs the pat on the back and who needs the kick in the pants at any given moment in their work. Do you know when to reward successful benchmark achievement or to prompt the actions that will lead to success? Catching people doing the right things is a leadership practice. Catching people missing the mark is a leadership discipline.

DECIDING AS A TEAM: IN TIMES OF UNCERTAINTY

There is a balance between knowing when to sit on the fence to gather more information and when you are forced to climb over the fence and make a swift decision. In the urgency of the moment, you aren't able to procrastinate, and you rarely have a clear-cut answer. Considering the options and risks is the hard task of leadership. Three tools can help in making decisions in times of uncertainty. Making good decisions is one of the main components of leadership, but it is a leadership competency not often enough included in leadership training. We make decisions every day. Some are routine, and some are consequential. In times of uncertainty, we aren't always given the luxury of time nor all the information needed when a decision must be made. Three overlapping ideas are insightful:

> » The bottom line defines *What* you are trying to do.

> » Decisions reflect *How* you will get there.

» The criteria behind your decisions clarify *Why* the particular decision was made.

How can you avoid expediency in a making too quick of a decision under pressure? The following tools will provide greater objectivity with less bias: The Ladder of Inference, Criteria Based Decisions, and Team Decision Making.

TOOL #1 - THE LADDER OF INFERENCE

The *Ladder of Inference* explains a sequence of thinking created by Chris Argyris and Peter Senge who collaborated on this insightful model. Argyris was an author and the James Bryant Conant Professor of Education and Organizational Behavior Emeritus at Harvard University. Senge is an American systems scientist and Senior Lecturer at the MIT Sloan School of Management. He is the author of *The Fifth Discipline: The Art & Practice of the Learning Organization.*[1] The Ladder of Inference is a decision-making tool that is widely used and discussed in the business world today. It describes the seven mental steps as you work your way up the ladder.

THE LADDER OF INFERENCE

Adapted from Chris Argyris and Peter Senge's Ladder of Inference. © theLDG.org

Each of the seven steps represent our typical way of thinking from the bottom of the ladder to the top.

OBSERVE – We observe things that we experience in daily life.

SELECT – We cannot pay attention to everything that we observe, so we make conscious choices of what to select and what to ignore based on our values and prior experience.

INTERPRET – We give personal meaning to what we decide to pay attention to.

ASSUMPTIONS – We make assumptions based on the meaning we give to all we observe.

CONCLUSIONS – We draw conclusions based on our prior beliefs.

BELIEFS – Our beliefs are formed based on both interpreted facts and prior beliefs.

ACTION – We decide and move forward based on both prior beliefs and conclusions.

This process can be a vicious cycle. The arrow on the right side of the ladder indicates that the beliefs we adopt will affect how we will likely filter facts the next time. As a result, we may not be considering all the relevant information, only the ones we choose as relevant in that moment.

AN EXAMPLE OF LADDER THINKING

You are meeting a potential business associate in your boardroom for lunch at Noon. They arrive late without apology or explanation. You conclude they don't value your time or professional courtesies. You decide based on these feelings that investing in this business relationship is not worth it because they don't respect you. This all happens before they even sit down at the boardroom table. When they suggest another meeting in two weeks, you make an excuse why that won't work with your schedule. They have no idea of your real feelings. If you had not run up the ladder as quickly as your mind and emotions led you, it might have crossed your mind that they were late for a valid reason. Yes, they could have explained and apologized, but you ignored that possibility and interpreted the meaning of their actions based on past experience, prior beliefs, and the data you selectively included in your thinking process. Beliefs reinforce the data you select to consider. Assumptions lead to conclusions.

Rather than going up Argyris and Senge's Ladder of Inference, consider a reflective process of going down the ladder. Ask yourself the following questions at each step to inform and intercept your intuition or gut reaction.

WHY – Could you choose another course of action? What are all the options?

BELIEF – Are your beliefs well founded? Do you have any bias in your thinking?

CONCLUSION – Is your conclusion rational and sound?

ASSUMPTIONS – Are your assumptions valid?

DATA – Have you selectively included data from what you have observed? What did you ignore?

FACTS – Are there other facts you should consider?

Ladder thinking will keep you from those intuitive gut decisions in a moment filled with emotions and selective past information that limits what you consider in the moment.

TOOL #2 - CRITERIA-BASED DECISIONS

The *Ladder of Inference* lets you honestly review your process of thinking that includes the beliefs, assumptions, and conclusions tied to a biased selection of data. The *Ladder of Inference* is a mindset you bring into decision-making moments. The *Decision Matrix* is a mathematical model that will help you objectify your decisions in light of the possibility of a biased mindset. Identifying the criteria that are most relevant and critical to your decision strengthens your final choice. A *Decision Matrix* will also help you prioritize the criteria you think are most important because they are not of equal value. The matrix is a simple table that visualizes the differences among your options. It brings quantitative objectivity to a final selection. Let's look at an example of how the matrix works in decision making. You are selecting a location for your annual offsite strategic planning. Start with a simple grid that indicates your three options and the three criteria most relevant to your final decision.

DECISION MATRIX

ANNUAL STRATEGIC PLANNING TEAM OFFSITE LOCATIONS				
Criteria:	Cost	Travel Options	Local Sites	Score
WEIGHTS				
Orlando, FL				
Key West, FL				
Naples, FL				

© theLDG.org

The three options include Orlando, Key West, and Naples. The top three criteria you have discussed and identified include cost, travel options, and local sites:

COST – budget limitations you need to stay within.

TRAVEL OPTIONS – accessibility, distance, and means of travel.

LOCAL SITES – the local attractions that will intrigue your team and their families who may join them.

Now it's time to use a simple 1 to 5 scale to evaluate each option. 1 = location rates poorly and 5 = location could not get any better.

ANNUAL STRATEGIC PLANNING TEAM OFFSITE LOCATIONS				
Criteria:	Cost	Travel Options	Local Sites	Score
WEIGHTS				
Orlando, FL	4	5	5	
Key West, FL	2	1	5	
Naples, FL	4	4	3	

This numerical summary is helpful but still doesn't get to the desired objectivity because it looks at all the criteria as being equally important. But are they? Most often your criteria in any decision are not of equal weight as it relates to the final choice. So, the next step in the *Decision Matrix* is to add a weight to each criterion. Again, using a 1 to 5 value, 1 = criterion is unimportant in your final decision and 5 = the criterion is highly important.

ANNUAL STRATEGIC PLANNING TEAM OFFSITE LOCATIONS				
Criteria:	Cost	Travel Options	Local Sites	Score
WEIGHTS	5	3	5	
Orlando, FL	4	5	5	
Key West, FL	2	1	5	
Naples, FL	4	4	3	

For the cost, 5 represents the reality of budget considerations. Travel Options gets a 3 because none of the locations represent complications of accessibility, travel time, or cost. The Local Sites gets a 5 because the extracurricular activities are important to family members who will also be attending. Now it's time to calculate the weighted values. Multiply the weighted value times each criterion value to get an adjusted score for each location.

ANNUAL STRATEGIC PLANNING TEAM OFFSITE LOCATIONS				
Criteria:	Cost	Travel Options	Local Sites	Score
WEIGHTS	5	3	5	
Orlando, FL	4x5=20	5x3=15	5x5=25	
Key West, FL	2x5=10	1x3=3	5x5=25	
Naples, FL	4x5=20	4x3=12	3x5=15	

Add the totals to each row for a final scoring.

ANNUAL STRATEGIC PLANNING TEAM OFFSITE LOCATIONS				
Criteria:	Cost	Travel Options	Local Sites	Score
WEIGHTS	5	3	5	
Orlando, FL	4x5=20	5x3=15	5x5=25	**60**
Key West, FL	2x5=10	1x3=3	5x5=25	**48**
Naples, FL	4x5=20	4x3=12	3x5=15	**47**

Your highest number is your preferred location. Orlando is the cheapest, least complicated to get to, and has an abundance of local attractions. The *Decision Matrix* helps avoid confusion, frustration, politics, bias, subjectivity, and gut reactions as you work though each step on the *Ladder of Influence* with an eye on essential criteria. What if you are working on a challenge that affects your entire team? How can you incorporate your team into the decision-making process with an understanding of how you can shorten the thinking process from insights in the *Ladder of Inference*? How can you use your team to determine the criteria, the weighting, and the values of your options? Let me repeat an earlier comment: *The Ladder of Inference* is a mindset you bring into decision making moments. The *Decision Matrix* is the process you can use in light of that mindset.

TOOL #3 - TEAM DECISIONS

There are four ways to decide with your team. Determine which option strategically fits your situation, the topic at hand, and the desired outcomes.

> #1 - I OWN IT. In some situations, the leader needs to be the one to decide, but the process to get to that decision invites all the input and feedback from your team and other stakeholders. Provide your best summary of the situation in question. Then listen to all perspectives. Analyze the insights, synthesize the information gathered, and use the *Decision Matrix* to quantify your decision. Once decided, report back and explain the reason for your decision.

> #2 - WE OWN IT – Option A. There are times and places for open discussion in which the leader is trying to read the group's mindset in an attempt to get to consensus. Consensus is a collective opinion where there is general agreement on a final decision. Use the *Decision Matrix* as a consensus tool with your team's insight on criteria, weight, and values.

> #3 - WE OWN IT – Option B. Consensus is not always possible given differing opinions and the intensity of commitment to those opinions. In more impassioned discussions, a decision might best be made by a simple majority vote or a two-thirds majority vote. The critical agreement, though, is that everyone supports the final decision even if it may not reflect their vote. Use the *Decision Matrix* to identify final scores, but let the team vote on a final decision in light of their reflection on the insight from the *Decision Matrix* process.

> #4 - YOU OWN IT. This last approach to making decisions as a team also includes extensive discussion with all stakeholders,

but the outcome-based decision is delegated to the team member who owns the area impacted by the decision. Their authority to make the final decision gets full support by the leader and the team. Give them full benefit of the team discussion. Either take the entire team through the matrix process or expect the assigned team member to use the team discussion to work through the matrix on their own. They should plan to report back with their rationale for their final choice.

.... 𝕐 ....

THE CORE

Three resources are available for more comprehensive and objective decision making: The Ladder of Inference, The Decision Matrix, and Team Decision Making. The Ladder of Inference is a mindset you bring into decision making moments. The Decision Matrix is the process you can use in light of that mindset. Involving your team is a way to create ownership and buy-in of the final decision.

REFLECTION QUESTION: If you could rewind your last major decision, would these tools have changed the outcome of what you decided?

COMPETENCE
MULTIPLIER #3

Leading Organizationally:
The Framework of Competence

◆

Every company has two organizational structures:
The formal one is written on the charts;
the other is the everyday relationship of the
men and women in the organization.

—HAROLD GENEEN
Former President of ITT Corporation

THE ORGANIZATIONAL BLUEPRINT: SEVEN BUILDING BLOCKS AND SEVEN RULES

Consider a logical order in the sequence of leading. Even though there is a connection among these, it is more dynamic than linear. Skipping any step negatively impacts each step that follows. This organizational framework provides the context for leadership development. Rate yourself on a scale from 1 to 10. 1 = you have not been intentional in articulating that building block and 10 = it's hard wired it into the thinking of every team member.

MISSION

Mission offers clarity on why your organization exists. It defines your company's business, its objectives, and its approach to achieving those objectives. Mission is your reason for being.

RULE #1 Never consider organizational Vision until you have absolute clarity on Mission.

VISION

What is your driving statement that continually re-casts a shared picture of what the organization is becoming? Vision stretches the organization's capacity and its self-image giving shape and direction to its future.

RULE #2 Never consider Values until you can clearly and compellingly cast Vision of what your company is becoming while living out the Mission.

VALUES

What are the guiding beliefs that influence how every team member thinks, talks, and behaves while living out the Mission on the way to achieving the Vision? Values translate into service standards. These statements reflect my idea of "behavioralizing" your values (which I discussed in the Introduction).

RULE #3 Never consider Strategy until you have described your organizational culture through shared behavioral Values. It is the values that describe how you will work together to achieve the Vision while living out the Mission.

Strategy

What are the steps that get the organization from where it is today to the next benchmark of achieving your organizational vision? Strategy incorporates best practice action plans to reach each milestone.

RULE #4 Never consider Structure until you have designed a Strategy to be skillfully executed by every team and every team member. Strategy plans the pathway from your current reality to your preferred future state or vision.

Structure

What is the most effective and efficient way to organize and maximize the resources of the organization? Structure is the framework needed for the strategy to fulfill the mission on the way to seeing the vision become reality.

RULE #5 Never plan for Staffing until you have designed the Structure that is being implemented to accomplish the Strategy.

Staffing

A change in Strategy leads to a change in Structure which results in a needed change in Staffing. Staffing models adapt to the structure that is required for the Strategy to be successful.

RULE #6 Never build Systems until you have thought through the Staffing that fits the structure in order to achieve the Strategy.

Systems

How do you streamline the organizational approach in optimizing the performance of every team member? Systems align individuals and teams around shared goals and facilitate collaboration across functional boundaries.

RULE #7 Once the Systems are in place, continue to revisit why you exist by telling organizational stories that illustrate the significance of your Mission and Vision.

THE CORE

Mission, Vision, and Values rarely, if ever, will change. Strategy, Structure, Staffing, and Systems will continue to change as the organization re-invents itself in response to a constantly changing business climate. Revisit the "Why" every thirty days as it will inevitably get fuzzy in the minds of your average team members. Being reminded of the "Why" makes continual change less traumatic for those same individuals.

REFLECTION QUESTION: Which of the seven rules need your review or revision in connecting to what preceded and what follows?

26

ALLOCATING LIMITED RESOURCES: STRATEGY AND STRATEGIC

What does it take to move an organization from today's realities toward the vision of a preferred future? Having a strategy and leading strategically are not the same. Remember, your leadership calling is to see what others do not yet see. The leadership challenge is finding the way to move forward incrementally. Strategic leaders determine the pathway with their teams fully engaged in the early discussions, potential solutions, and final decisions, while never hesitating to be the voice that initiates, clarifies, and leads to consensus or conclusions.

BUSINESS STRATEGY

Rich Horwath, author of *Deep Dive: The Proven Method for Building Strategy, Focusing Your Resources, and Taking Smart Action*, said, "Business strategy is the intelligent allocation of limited resources through a unique system of activities to outperform the competition in serving customers."[1]

INTELLIGENT. Strategy is grounded in fact more than in feeling. Are you capturing the right metrics to make mindful decisions?

ALLOCATION. Strategy determines what resources are applied to specific tactics that lead to anticipated outcomes.

LIMITED. Strategy recognizes that every organization needs more resources than it currently has. The greater abundance of resources available, the less strategic an organization may become.

UNIQUE. Strategy identifies what sets you apart from others. Your unique system of activities determines your branding and tells your story in the marketplace.

OUTPERFORM. Strategy recognizes the need to know the competition better than they know themselves. It identifies the essential criteria needed for honest comparisons within your industry.

SERVING. Strategy recognizes that the customer is always right. It necessitates the quality control of products or services while listening to the candid voice of the average customer.

THE CORE

It's as simple as this: Strategy is the noun. Strategic is the adjective. Always be intentional with how you use and spend your resources.

REFLECTION QUESTIONS: Do you know the actual realities of where you are today? How broadly (externally) and how deeply (internally) are you listening in order to determine that reality? Do you have informed clarity on the final destination of your preferred future? How will you involve all team members to determine the strategy to move from here to there? Will you do whatever is required to sustain the vision, mission, and especially the values that define organizational culture while executing your strategy?

A Meeting Rhythm: Communicating with Clarity and Consistency

The consensus about meetings from almost everyone is that you have too many and they are the biggest time waster in your workday. It's assumed and accepted that we must meet, and yet meetings are not often productive enough in moving us from our current state to the preferred future state. So, do we need to meet? Why? Can we change the outcome so the meeting is more worthwhile and intentional? The essential purpose of meetings is for consistent communication among relevant stakeholders in the pursuit of: (1) providing updated information, (2) clarifying relevant questions or challenges, (3) collaborating on solutions, and (4) identifying next steps, including what specific actions are needed next, who's responsible, and when reports are due.

Meetings with Different Purposes

In working with teams on this topic, I often describe a variety of meeting types. Then I pose the question: What kind of meetings does your team need in order to maximize your productivity? I put them into smaller work groups to discuss and bring back a proposal to the entire group. Then we collate their ideas into a Team Meeting Plan.

PURPOSE - Clarify the purpose of each type of meeting connected to shared strategy.

OUTCOMES - Anticipate the outcomes that are needed to stay on track with the project management plan.

ESSENTIAL - Identify the essential team members whose participation is critical. Secondary stakeholders can provide feedback ahead of time as well as get a copy of the action plan resulting from the meeting.

WHEN - How long and how often? Meetings don't need to be monthly or weekly or an entire hour.

FORMAT - In person or virtual? During the Covid-19 pandemic, we all got a big dose of virtual meetings! We learned how they can be a useful tool when in-person meetings are not possible. For virtual meetings, use video technology to visibly engage those who tend to multi-task in audio-only meetings.

A MENU OF MEETINGS

THE "MOMENT-IN-TIME" HUDDLE. The daily or weekly catch up. Short, sweet, and to the point.

THE INTENTIONAL BENCHMARK GATHERING. The weekly or biweekly check in on action plan assignments and deadlines.

THE STRATEGIC REVIEW AND ASSESSMENT. The monthly or quarterly update with adjustments and revisions to the project management plan.

THE MISSION-VISION APPRAISAL. The annual perspective to determine strategic plan revisions needed in moving from where you are today to where you want to be at the end of next year.

THE LOOK AROUND THE CORNER PERSPECTIVE. Every three-five years or more often if needed, ask what business you are in, or should be in. Then ask what you need to do differently in response to a changing customer, market, competition, advancements in technology, past mistakes.

THE CORE

Use your meeting rhythm to keep asking and answering these core questions. Start by letting your team weigh in on the kinds of meetings most needed to reach your shared goals.

REFLECTION QUESTIONS: The Context Question: What did we used to do? The Reality Question: What are we doing today? The Change Question: What should we do differently? The Priority Question: What should we do next? The Letting Go Question: What should we stop doing?

28

LEADING IN A CRISIS: WHEN EVERYTHING GOES WRONG

In his writing about good to great companies, Jim Collins discovered the "Stockdale Paradox." In his book, *Good to Great: Why Some Companies Make the Leap and Others Don't,* Collins explains, "It didn't matter how bleak the situation...they all maintained unwavering faith that they would not just survive but prevail as a great company. And yet, at the same time, they became relentlessly disciplined at confronting the most brutal facts of their current reality."[1] Crisis leadership maintains that your prevailing attitude alongside your innate personal drive will confront the obstacles standing in your way.

Bill George served as CEO at Medtronic, a global leader in medical technology, services, and solutions. In 2009, he published 7 *Lessons for Leading in a Crisis*[2] at the outset of the economic crisis at that time. George frames four foundational questions for leaders in times of crisis:

1. Is this crisis your defining moment?

2. Are you prepared to step up and lead?

3. Can you stay on your "True North" course, no matter how great the pressures or temptations?

4. How can you make a difference in the world...which is the ultimate fulfillment of leading in a crisis?[3]

Once you answer those foundational questions, what are the actions that follow? I propose the following seven ways to navigate times of crisis whether from an internal or external cause.

STEP INTO THE UNCERTAINTY OF THE CRISIS AND CONTINUE LEADING. The best of education never fully prepares you for the realities that continue to unfold and change in times of industry crisis, company crisis, personal crisis, national crisis, or global crisis.

COMMUNICATE THROUGHOUT THE JOURNEY. Share the learning journey you are on without having all the details that will be available when your critics show up to tell you what you should have done. Schedule a daily briefing (or as often as is needed) to share new information and implications of that new information.

EMPATHIZE AUTHENTICALLY. Talk about the anxiety, fear, or panic everyone is feeling. Your identification of valid emotions makes it safe for others to be courageously transparent. Remind everyone that we are not alone in this journey; we are doing it together.

CLARIFY WHAT'S TRUE. What are the plans and priorities for the things that are in your control as you understand them? Indicate the reasons why. Be honest about the obstacles and celebrate the small wins. The urgency of the situation will help you align all resources toward a great solution.

BE OPEN. It is the unknown that feeds insecurity. Admit when your trial and error approach has led you to a dead end. Don't hide it. Don't explain it away. Don't blame others. Leverage all this learning to clarify next steps.

PHASE THE WAY OUT. Think and act in phases: Immediate realities, key decisions, benchmarks, solution scenarios, game plan, next steps, and outcomes.

REFLECT TO CAPTURE INSIGHTS. Debrief on what was learned through mistakes, key insights, identification of emerging leaders, and resources needed for the next crisis.

THE CORE

Plan now for your next crisis. What do you know about crisis situations? What will you wish you had addressed before the immediate reality? Who will be on your crisis management team? What values will guide your crisis decisions?

REFLECTION QUESTIONS: What are the brutal facts of that new reality? How is it affecting your employees, customers, vendors, and investors? Are you asking each stakeholder group or just assuming? What needs to change in how you will get work done? What resources are needed to make those changes? How will you lead differently to sustain your market share? How can you outpace your competition because of your agility? How are you ranking your To Do list? What is the next step you will take?

Leadership shows judgment, wisdom,
personal appeal, and proven competence.

—WALT DISNEY,
American Entrepreneur

PART THREE

CORE CAPACITY

Not how smart you are, but how high can you lead with the smarts you already have?

CAPACITY MULTIPLIER #1: PERSONAL DRIVE

CAPACITY MULTIPLIER #2: ORGANIZATIONAL ENABLERS

CORE CAPACITY: THE PATHWAY TO LEADERSHIP POTENTIAL

◆

Leadership is the capacity to translate vision into reality.

—WARREN G. BENNIS
American Scholar, Organizational Consultant, and Author

The Shadow Side of Leadership Capacity: Can I? Should I? Must I?

Let's start with a definition of terms:

» LEADERSHIP – the alignment of positive influence (character) and effective action (competence).

» CAPACITY – the ability to lead effectively and efficiently in your current role with the potential and readiness to lead at higher levels of responsibility within the organization.

» DEVELOPMENT – the life-long commitment to continually learn and apply new understandings of how to incrementally improve yourself, your team, and your organization.

» CAN I – the combination of character and competence required for the current role.

» SHOULD I – assessing if it is the right season in life to take on a leadership role with greater responsibility.

» MUST I – even if I can and I should, must I pursue or accept a role at a higher level of responsibility and complexity?

CAN I?

The question of capacity is tied to self-awareness and self-discovery. What is your own assessment, or that of others, whether you have the capacity to lead effectively and efficiently in your current role or in a higher role? If you have that additional capacity then either: (1) ask for stretch assignments in your current role, or (2) consider new opportunities at a higher employment category. If you don't have that capacity in terms of readiness for your current role or a higher role, then (1) find a role that fits your current skillset, (2) identify an internal or external mentor or coach to help you close the gap, and (3) create a personal development plan that identifies the competencies and resources you need to help you learn and apply new skills.

SHOULD I?

There are times when you do possess the training, experience, and competence to consider or pursue a role that would take on more complicated and demanding responsibilities. Then there are seasons of life when you might hesitate to add more commitments to an overloaded life without much margin. If you are already stressed, more responsibility will only compound negatively the impact on everything you do and everyone around you at work and at home. Life with a new baby and continual sleepless nights is not a time to take on more. Caring for aging parents with all their healthcare needs and appointments is the right thing to do to honor them, but it's not the season to stretch in new ways at work. Other considerations include chronic sickness in the family, showing priority to your spouse's opportunity for promotion, financial stressors, relational dysfunctions within your immediate household, etc. You get the idea that it is smart to do a whole-of-life assessment when seeking or accepting a promotion.

Must I?

If you have the capacity to pursue or consider an advanced position, do you have a choice whether or not to move forward? If you are in your sweet spot professionally and love what you do and those you work with, why would you give that up? The motivators to move up to an advanced role are more money, prestige, or power. Remember, the danger of the *Peter Principle* is always a threat. What if you advance to a level of incompetence? The criteria to use in answering the "Must I" question includes analyzing your fit in the current role in the following areas: competence, organizational culture and values, team dynamics, efficiency in doing a job you know, reporting relationships, salary and benefits, and opportunity for stretch assignments. The same criteria will apply to your due diligence in considering a new role where some of those factors are yet unknown. Must I? No! But what are the unintended consequences of making that decision one way or the other? If you pass up an offer, will you be sidelined by the organization for future consideration? The question is not easy to answer.

When Competence Limits Capacity

Our leadership strengths can have a downside even when we can, should, and must. The downside comes from an overuse of competence. This means that we might overdo the things we think we can, should, and must do to the point of negatively affecting our leadership capacity. The development agenda for every leader goes by many names: skills, competencies, capabilities, strengths, abilities, capacity, talent, etc. Let me use a personal example to demonstrate the shadow side of one of my strengths. One of my talent themes in the Clifton StrengthsFinder is "Activator."[1] It implies that I have the potential to develop this talent into a leadership strength much more so than many of the other thirty-four talent themes. Activator describes someone who is "impatient for action." Activators are great on a team as they constantly push to get things done. An Activator might say at the end of a long discussion, "Let's not table this for another meeting. Let's make the best decision with today's information. If we need to circle back and revisit the decision, then we can do that at our next meeting."

What's the Downside?

Activators can move to final decisions prematurely, and that can be the shadow side of this strength that limits one's leadership capacity. Their impatience can cause them to move ahead before it is needed or before all the facts are in. Gallup describes the downside of Activators as those who: "speak before they think, can be a loose cannon, and follow the sequence of *ready, fire, aim.*" The Activator hits the "send" button on an email before the thinking side of the brain catches up to the feeling side of the brain. They are prone to make impulsive expedient judgements about an individual, an idea, a problem, or a solution.

Capacity Reflection for the Impulsive Leader

Gaining wisdom from experience necessitates reflection which is an investment in understanding the situation. Reflection invites us to take time to consider all the causes and consequences prior to taking action. It moves the leader beyond reacting to a situation to allow for a more measured response. Some capacity reflective questions for the impulsive leader:

- » RUSH. What's the rush? Why am I in a hurry on this?

- » RISK. What's the risk? What might I lose if I'm wrong?

- » WISDOM. Am I really acting wisely in this action? Am I being stubborn and impulsive?

- » ASSUMPTIONS. Am I making unfair assumptions? What am I taking for granted?

- » BIAS. Am I taking action based on presuppositions that may or may not be correct?

- » OPTIONS. What are all of my options? Why am I not weighing all the alternatives according to agreed-upon criteria that has been weighted appropriately.

- » VALUES. Does my conclusion reflect my personal values as well as the values that define our organizational culture?

- » MODEL. What am I modeling for our emerging leaders?

The "Can I" or "Should I" or "Must I" questions will guide you through the shadow side of leadership capacity. There may be a better time, or you may need to address the leadership competence or behavior gaps that will be central in a new or expanded opportunity. Are you willing to put in the effort to close the gap and enhance your leadership capacity?

THE ORGANIZATIONAL ROI: THE CASE FOR CAPACITY-BASED LEADERSHIP

Regarding the distinction between *competence* and *capacity*, it is fitting to offer a clarification in discussing the case for capacity-based leadership.

COMPETENCE represents a specific set of leadership skills needed for efficient and effective practice given the strategic outcomes of one's role and the cultural context of the organization's values.

CAPACITY is the level of organizational complexity at which one's competence can be applied.

CAPACITY begs the question of one's ability to lead in areas of greater responsibility.

COMPETENCE is your set of leadership skills.

CAPACITY is what you do with those skills to continue to add increasing value in leading at higher levels of complexity and responsibility.

CAPACITY represents the *productive potential* of any team member, team, department, division, or organization. The more each leader's capacity is developed and maximized, the more it increases the potential for greater productivity throughout the entire organization. Why are some leaders ready to step into positions with greater complexity, responsibility, and risk? Can leaders develop specific competencies in order to extend their leadership capacity? Consider seven *Capacity Amplifiers* and ask yourself the capacity question embedded in each factor.

1. BASICS. Consider both your IQ and your EQ. IQ is the ability and speed at which you acquire information including analyzing and synthesizing that information for critical thinking and strategic execution. EQ is the awareness and the management of your emotional response to the events and people around you. It is being savvy in all the interpersonal relationships that have an emotional dimension or exchange. Neither high IQ with low EQ nor high EQ with low IQ will enhance your capacity. They work hand in hand.

   ...*Capacity Question*: Are you assuming EQ while you leverage IQ?

2. PERSONAL WIRING. Review your profile on any number of assessments that indicate personality style, competency strengths, value-based motivators, or career derailers. Your profile represents a blending of skills, behaviors, and tendencies that may or may not lend themselves to leading in roles with greater complexity. Leadership leverages one's strengths while managing one's non-strength areas to find the best fit and make the greatest contribution to the organization.

   ...*Capacity Question:* Do you know your profile?

3. SEASON OF LIFE. If balance provides a healthy goal for any leader, then some seasons of life are more conducive to increased leadership responsibility than others. Seasons are defined by age of children, needs of aging parents, healthcare crises, financial stressors, family relationship challenges, required geographical relocation, and as you know, there can be many other factors.

   ...*Capacity Question:* What season are you in?

4. PROFESSIONAL DRIVE. Some personalities are more driven, more competitive, and more committed to continual professional development. Greater capacity is the result of that drive to lead at higher levels of organizational complexity by maximizing one's wiring and current season of life.

…*Capacity Question:* How driven are you?

5. WORKPLACE CHALLENGE. The *70-20-10 Rule* suggests that 70 percent of your capacity development is the result of having a challenging work assignment that stretches core competencies needed for increased responsibility. The challenge will motivate those with the professional drive to push the limits of their leadership capacity to a new benchmark.

…*Capacity Question:* How challenged are you in your current role?

6. INTENTIONAL LEARNING. 10 percent of the *70-20-10 Rule* represents an investment in research-based assessments and 360-degree feedback to provide insight into specific areas of leadership where additional learning and application are essential. That information provides the foundation to create a professional development growth plan to increase competence.

…*Capacity Question:* Will you invest in assessments and open the door to 360-degree feedback from your direct reports, peers, and senior leaders to establish a learning plan for further growth and development?

7. ACCOUNTABLE COACHING. An internal or external coach can provide a voice of accountability to monitor, measure, and manage your professional development growth

plan. This is 20 percent of the *70-20-10 Rule*. Coaching will not only focus your efforts but also accelerate the expansion of your leadership capacity.

> ...*Capacity Question:* Would you consider investing in an executive coach as your career development advocate?

These seven leadership *Capacity Amplifiers* will help you determine if and when you pursue or accept increased responsibilities that demand more skills and more time than your current role requires. Are you driven to maximize your capacity by identifying and addressing the leadership behavior and leadership skill gaps that are currently limiting your capacity? So how does one maximize the drive for greater capacity that leads to leadership potential? Two capacity multipliers provide a guide for the motivated leader: Personal Drive (Chapters 29-35) and Organizational Enablers (Chapters 36-42).

*The capacity of a leader increases
when they say no to the wrong things
and yes to the right things.*

CAPACITY
MULTIPLIER #1

*Personal Drive: Desire and Effort in
Achieving Professional Goals*

························· ◆ ·························

*In the good-to-great companies, it didn't matter
how bleak the situation…they all maintained
unwavering faith that they would not just survive
but prevail as a great company. And yet, at the
same time, they became relentlessly disciplined
at confronting the most brutal facts of
their current reality.*

—JIM COLLINS
Author of *Good to Great*

STARTING POINT: CALLING, CAPACITY, DEVELOPMENT

There is an assumed myth that most senior leadership roles are too complex for "just anyone." The truth is that most people do lead sometime, somewhere, and somehow. When leadership opportunities occur, those who succeed are the ones who connect positive influence (the relationship-oriented soft skills of leading) to effective action (the results-oriented hard skills of leading). In the end, they get the job done at home, at work, or somewhere in the community at large. If they reflect on what just happened, they may stop long enough to realize how to do the same thing more efficiently and more effectively the next time. This is leadership in its earliest stages. It is the starting point of leadership development.

CALLING. Some will quickly discover that they have a tendency to be in a leading role and feel committed to developing their leadership skill set even further. Success in the simple leadership assignments becomes a calling for some to grow and develop the competencies and the behaviors required by other more complicated challenges. Mark Twain said, "The two most important days in your life are the day you were born and the day you found out why." Leadership may be your "why."

CAPACITY. Leadership capacity asks the question, "How high can you lead in the organization?" Capacity increases as you invest your (1) Potential by taking on more challenging job assignments, (2) Performance by consistently surpassing expected outcomes, and (3) Personal Drive in the intensity of the leadership interest within you. Capacity varies by the leader's season of life as well as the company's season of organizational development.

DEVELOPMENT. Leadership development is that lifelong commitment to never stop learning about leadership. It's not about the identity of the leader. It's about connecting the right competencies to the needs of the organization in order to achieve strategic outcomes. It involves working with and working through a team of people to consistently achieve those outcomes while sustaining the important values that define the culture of the company.

THE CORE

The starting point is a recognition that you often find yourself in leading positions by your initiative or by the request of others. When there is a sense of fulfillment, you may be motivated to learn how to lead more effectively and efficiently.

REFLECTION QUESTIONS: Do you have what is required for success in a new assignment? Do you have the time, resources, and ability to close the competency gap in your leadership growth agenda in light of what will be needed in this new challenge? Can you recruit and align others who will fill in those gaps? What is the career significance if you succeed? Is there a cost of failure to the company or to you professionally? Should you pass on this opportunity and wait for a better fit? Do you feel compelled to increase your leadership capacity?

EXECUTIVE PRESENCE: IT'S ALL ABOUT PERCEPTIONS

Leadership is about influence. Influence depends on your reputation, and reputation starts with first impressions. It may not be fair, but how we are initially perceived by others either strengthens or inhibits the executive presence that others hope to see in leaders. Harvard Business School professor and social psychologist, Amy Cuddy, has been studying this topic with colleagues. Take time for her TED Talk and her book, *Presence: Bringing Your Boldest Self to your Biggest Challenges.*[1] Cuddy reminds every leader that team members are always interpreting two questions: (1) Can they trust you, and (2) Can they respect you? Psychologists refer to these as *warmth* (trustworthiness) and *competence* (respect). Leaders too often conclude that competence is the most important, but in Cuddy's research, warmth is the most telling factor in how people judge your reputation. So how do you get past the first impressions to let people see your warmth as well as your competence.

VISUALLY. Initial impressions are closely connected to dress, posture, hygiene, gestures, and body language. Dress is unique and is tied to the culture of the organization. Some are more formal. Many are less formal. A rule of thumb is to upgrade your dress a notch at first. Then settle into what is the range of organizational norms in terms of style or formality.

VOCALLY. People measure you by vocabulary or word choice, awareness of industry acronyms, volume, pause, pace, and regional accents, but remember your non-verbals almost always speak more loudly than your words.

CAPACITY. Your leadership mindset, skills, and behaviors should not be overlooked. For some, it's where their executive presence challenge begins. How high can you lead? What are the factors that influence the perception of your executive presence?

HOW TO DEVELOP AN EXECUTIVE REPUTATION

Leaders often talk too much when they should be the best question asker in the room. Executive leadership has as much to do with asking the right questions as is does with having the right answers. The Right Question Institute says it this way: "Questioning is the ability to organize our thinking around what we don't know."[2] Fourth Century Greek philosopher, Socrates, suggested that we ask and answer questions to foster critical thinking and make complex ideas more understandable. His approach was to probe a possible solution by asking continual questions to see if a contradiction was eventually identified. Executives pursue a line of thinking for the same reason. If contradictions are identified in potential explanations or solutions, they move on to the next consideration in problem solving. Executives learn to ask powerful questions. They should start with What, How, Who, When, Where questions before ever asking a Why question. The Why questions always put people on the defensive. Let's think about how your questions can be more productive.

1. Don't ask multiple choice questions. Ask short questions with a singular focus: *Tell me one thing you learned? What was the result?*

2. Don't ask leading questions. Don't hint at your anticipated answer. *Do you think it's a marketing problem?*

3. Don't ask closed questions prompting only yes or no answers. *Does the sales team understand our customer?*

4. Do ask your question again in a different way if no answer is immediately given: *Let me ask it this way.*

5. Do repeat the answer you get in your own words to confirm accurate understanding. *This is what I heard you say. Is that correct?*

6. Do follow up with questions that probe deeper. *If you were our customer, what would be your expectation?*

Learning to ask thoughtful questions while listening for honest answers contributes to the perception of an executive leader's warmth and competence. What if your approach to creating a positive executive reputation in the way you are perceived by others was tied to what you asked rather than what you said? Yes, it is counterintuitive, but that is what might distinguish you from every other leader in your organization. *That* is executive presence.

THE CORE

Change the perception and change the reputation. Change the reputation and change the influence. Executive presence is how others perceive you. How you show up and how you sound are the initial criteria used by others. Eventually, the perception is defined by the balance of how much people like you and how much they respect you. Err on one side or the other and it damages your reputation. They work hand in hand. A starting place is your ability to ask great questions. It can be as simple as asking, "What do I need to know from you today?" Asking powerful questions is hard work because it takes preparation. Start with Andrew Finlayson's *Questions That Work*. It's an entire book of questions for various work situations.

REFLECTION QUESTIONS: Do you have the ability to present yourself displaying a self-confidence that you can handle uncertain times and take charge of difficult and unpredictable challenges? Can you make daunting decisions in a short time with incomplete information? Can you stand firm in conversations with your executive peers?

DUE DILIGENCE: DO YOUR HOMEWORK

Lifelong learning is the commitment of sustaining leaders. When you stop learning, you stop growing. When you stop growing, you stop leading effectively. What is on your learning agenda? In what areas will your due diligence prepare you for each new leadership crossroad and the decisions that are to be answered?

THREE APPRAISALS

1. KEEP LEARNING ABOUT YOURSELF.

Continue to identify your own leadership competency gaps. As your role changes, so does the prioritization of specific competencies needed for effective leadership. Three sources of information will help you identify gaps in each of those competency areas.

REFLECTION. Consider your own reflective assessment of where you are, where you are going, and what is needed to get there.

FEEDBACK. 360-degree feedback from select stakeholders will add to the understanding of blind spots. This includes what others know about you that you are not in touch with. Blind Spots can interfere with your effectiveness as a leader, and these negative characteristics become an elephant in the room for your team. Since unsolicited feedback can make you defensive, be open and courageous by asking for feedback. When you initiate by asking for feedback, it changes the dynamic for the team and for the leader.

ASSESSMENTS. Research-based leadership competency assessments will complete the review. Feedback will often provide the anecdotal examples of information that shows up in a more formal assessment tool. Out of all that insight, you can develop a learning plan to expand your capacity in each gap identified. Consider joining (or creating) a professional learning community to process your understanding, your internalization of the value, and your application of new practices in each competency. Executive coaching can provide the accountability and the resources to keep learning while you apply new insights that foster new leadership habits.

2. KEEP LEARNING ABOUT YOUR TEAM.

Leaders with a coaching mindset help teams maximize the collaborative benefit of working together. That implies leadership on two parallel tracks.

TEAMS. Keep leading your teams. What are their interpersonal obstacles to become a high-performing team? Do they value the contribution each person brings? Do they know how to manage the emotional interchanges? Can they leverage conflict around ideas to generate innovative solutions without making it personal? Do you recognize their achievements and celebrate their accomplishments? Do they have the resources needed to meet strategic goals in the timeline expected?

TEAM MEMBERS. Keep leading your team members. Does each person have clarity on their assignment? Do they get to work out of their strengths most of the time? If not, might they make a more substantive contribution in a different assignment? Do they have the drive, time, and resources to develop the strengths that directly connect to identified strategic outcomes? Are they rewarded appropriately to recognize exceptional performance? Develop individuals and you will develop teams. Develop teams and you will develop the organization.

3. KEEP LEARNING ABOUT YOUR ORGANIZATION.

Sustaining leaders understand the organizational development life cycle, including the normal and predictable challenges and opportunities reflected in each stage of that cycle. Leaders are strategic in knowing how and when to communicate and address the opportunity or the challenge. Leaders analyze the relevant data to see around the corner of what's coming.

ENGAGE EMPLOYEES. Leaders are committed to engage employees at every level to solve the challenge or build on the opportunity. Leadership at the organizational level focuses on broad culture transformation. That implies a leadership competency profile to effectively shape corporate culture that addresses both the normal and the predictable challenges in your current stage of organizational maturity.

REVIEW THE BASICS. When you review the mission, vision, and values, has anything changed? If so, strategy is re-evaluated. Remember, the need for a revised strategy leads to revisiting the structure, staffing, and systems needed to accomplish the strategy.

THE CORE

Organizations are always changing in response to the market, the competition, and the technology. Sustaining leaders anticipate those changes, communicate the reason behind the changes, and lead individuals and teams to manage the transition that follows each change event. The more you know about yourself, your team members, and your organization, the more effective you will be in your efforts to revisit and revise the strategy to successfully fulfill your mission, vision, and values.

REFLECTION QUESTIONS: When is the last time you evaluated the alignment among your mission, vision, values, strategy, structure, staffing, and systems? Will you commit to dedicating time in the near future for this important exercise?

AN UNEXPECTED GIFT: FORGIVENESS

Forgiveness is a gift. Leaders model this by owning and dealing with their own mistakes or failures. They share their own story and the lessons learned to move forward in a better way as a result of what they discovered about themselves. Then leaders are also willing to forgive team members who make mistakes. The leadership assignment is to help that team member learn from their mistake or failure as an opportunity to continue their personal development. Recently, I posted this topic for discussion with my LinkedIn group of global leadership practitioners. Their insights were profound and have helped shape my own thinking about my own encounters with failure. When failure is unacceptable and forgiveness in not given, leaders and team members will get stuck in the unintended consequences including stress, anxiety, lower self-confidence, lack of trust in future actions, lack of trust from team members, decline in self-respect and integrity, and an increase in personal shame. It is far better when we can help each other benefit from mistakes and can view them as learning opportunities to strengthen the individual, the team, and the entire organization.

OWN YOUR FAILURE. Ask for help if needed, apologize to everyone touched by your mistake, make restitution when it's needed, let it go, and reflect on what you have learned. More important than greater understanding or illustration is the application to yourself and each imperfect team member. Yes, we are all imperfect!

LEVERAGE YOUR FAILURE. Build trust with team members by designing a culture where mistakes and failure are part of the learning process in order to do things differently moving forward. When you pay it forward, your response to missteps models healthy failure leadership for how your direct reports lead their own direct reports. The trickle-down lessons acknowledge that mistakes happen, but rather than blame and shame, leaders focus on learning for everyone's benefit.

AVOID CHRONIC FAILURE. Repeated failure can be a sign of the wrong person in the wrong position. It may document the need for retraining, reassignment, or even release and replacement. Each of those choices necessitates honest conversations with the team member to seek shared agreement on next steps. Professional counsel can be beneficial to address root causes in situations of chronic failure. Even if you need to terminate the individual, why not provide them an opportunity to find healing and health in order to move on? It's a gift that represents the best of leadership and organizations that care.

THE CORE

So, what leadership mistake do you keep stumbling over? Why
is it so hard for you to accept the same forgiveness you offer
to others? An executive coach may help you find your way
through this, but more realistically, you may want to invest
your time with a professional who can help you get to the root
causes that shed light in a way to help you move forward with
a freedom not otherwise possible.

REFLECTION QUESTIONS: Failure can be a career derailer or it
can be a learning experience that leads to greater leadership capacity.
Thomas Edison said, "I haven't failed. I've just found 10,000 ways
that don't work." For what failure do you need to forgive yourself? Is
there need for apology or restitution? Which member of your team
needs the gift of forgiveness?

LEADING FROM ANY CHAIR: SECOND CHAIR HAS INFLUENCE

Recently, one of my LinkedIn contacts in The Leadership Development Group, asked an intriguing leadership question: "Do you need a position or a title to be a leader?" My leadership definition is not that complicated. Leadership is the ever-changing fulcrum point that balances positive influence and effective action. It's easy to rationalize away the importance of the soft skills when you are overwhelmed with the demand for effective action. Both are essential. There are people in any organization who have mastered the balance of both. They work without titles or positions or assigned parking or an office with a door, and they are both influential and effective in the actions they accomplish. They are the hidden leaders who may only sit in a support role as second chair. When their character supports their competence, it enhances their influence and expands the capacity of the entire organization.

LEADING FROM ANY CHAIR

The most inspirational TED Talk, in my opinion, is Ben Zander's "The Transformative Power of Classical Music."[1] It reflects his leadership insights from years as Conductor of the Boston Philharmonic Orchestra. My dad would be surprised at my admission after his own lifetime love of the classics. It took me nearly a lifetime to understand it in the way Zander convincingly explains. The TED Talk gives a glimpse of Zander's insights into leaders who possess both positive influence and effective action. In 2000, Ben and Rosamund Zander published their best-selling book, *The Art of Possibility: Transforming Professional and Personal Life.*[2] Chapter Five, "Leading from Any Chair," answers the leadership question posed in the opening paragraph of this chapter. Ben tells the story of a cellist in his orchestra who found herself sitting in the eleventh chair in a section of twelve. She was devastated as if that chair was insignificant. Ben understood. He kept reaching out to her until she finally offered an approach to playing a section of a symphony in their repertoire. Her great ideas made an impression on the entire orchestra.

Since that day, the authors explained, the cellist played like a completely different person. Not only did she continue to be technically perfect, but her playing and her presence rose to a new level of contribution. She discovered that she could influence the entire orchestra even from the eleventh chair! Wherever people sit in your organization's hierarchy, they have the potential to offer innovation, solutions, and new directions. When they realize their voice is being heard and they have an opportunity to contribute, their employee satisfaction and employee engagement is motivated by their own intrinsic drive and passion. They discover they have influence and are effective in their actions. They are leading without title or position. When second chair or eleventh chair starts to lead, they exponentially multiply the productive potential of the organization and the capacity of every other leader.

THE CORE

Do you value the insight of everyone in your organization? Do you acknowledge the importance of their voice? Do you collect the ideas of people in every cubicle and work area in your company? When you do, you have expanded your leadership capacity exponentially! You have an informed number of leaders in your organization who may never have a title, but they are by definition, leaders. They come to work most days and combine influence and action to try to make your company one of the best places to work!

REFLECTIVE QUESTION: When is the last time you wandered around your company with the only agenda of noticing, acknowledging, and listening when you ask: "If you could change anything around here, what would you change?"

FIVE QUESTIONS: WHEN DID YOU LAST ASK...?

The most important leadership assignment is an invitation to regularly step away from operations to the quiet place of organizational diagnosis. It is a contemplative process that is more about thinking than talking. It's more about a pause than a plan. It's more about reflection than results.

No one will schedule your time for contemplative reflection. Don't miss these moments only assigned to leaders with responsibility for strategy. Busy? Yes! Exhausted? Yes! Dealing with the urgent? Yes! Looking for the next *silver bullet* that promises to solve all your challenges? Yes?

Spending regularly scheduled time in personal reflection will lead you to an understanding of two competing ideas: (1) The *important* compared to the *urgent* (2) The *priority* compared to the *chaos*. Both will gain greater clarity as you ask these five perplexing questions that no one can start answering except you. Taking time out to reflect starts with five questions that are central to your organization's productive potential? Answering these questions will generate insights and data needed for analysis of your current realities in order to articulate next steps on the way to a preferred future.

ASKING THE RIGHT QUESTIONS IS AS IMPORTANT AS GETTING THE RIGHT ANSWERS

The CONTEXT Question:
What did we used to do?

The REALITY Question:
What are we doing today?

The CHANGE Question:
What should we be doing differently?

The PRIORITY Question:
What should we be doing next?

The LETTING GO Question:
What should we stop doing?

Applying Your Answers

Leadership capacity is a process of incremental change: One *behavior* at a time. One *competency* at a time. Twentieth Century American mathematician, Richard Hamming, illustrated the compounding value of incremental change. His work had many insights for computer engineering and telecommunications. He said, "Knowledge and productivity are like compound interest. The more you know, the more you learn; the more you learn, the more you can do; the more you can do, the more the opportunity...Given two people with exactly the same ability, the one person who manages day in and day out to get in one more hour of thinking will be tremendously more productive over a lifetime." Every time you stop to ask one of the five questions you are creating moments of learning, knowing, and doing more. Start asking. Start thinking. Start making time to focus on the important and the priority rather than the urgent and the chaos.

THE CORE

Some leaders have the organizational assignment to think strategically about where the company is today and where it needs to be in eighteen or twenty-four months. A personal offsite scheduled on your calendar will provide the time and place to leave operations behind and spend an entire day analyzing the most relevant data. Use the five questions to get started. Spend an hour on each one. Sit, think, look at the hard data, dream, write notes, and then take the remaining hours to draft a strategy reflection. This is not a strategic plan, but it is strategic thinking. Perhaps it is only a list of observations in response to each of the five questions. Those observations will contribute to the effectiveness and efficiency of achieving your productive potential!

REFLECTION QUESTIONS: What if you could invest minimal time and resources to increase your leadership capacity by 5 percent. Would you do it? The *D.W.Y.S.Y.W.G.T.D.* acronym is impossible to pronounce, so just consider the words: *Do What You Said You Were Going to Do!* When will you ask the five questions? When will you guide your team to ask the questions? Will you let them answer with their authentic perspective?

NINE BOX
REVISITED:
PERFORMANCE,
POTENTIAL, AND
PERSONAL DRIVE

Leadership capacity is understood in the quadrant model of the
Performance Potential Matrix which is a variation of the *Nine Box Grid*.
As you consider your team members, in which quadrant would you
place each one? It is a subjective process, but critical to maximize
the capacity of your collective team. One challenge is how to retain
those with high potential and high performance: the upper right
quadrant. At the other end of the continuum, how do you deal with
the low performer with low potential: the lower left quadrant. How

do you respond to the underperformer? As a leader, the more you maximize the contribution of each direct report, the more you increase your own capacity to give more attention to strategy that goes beyond daily operations. Team members in each quadrant need a unique message from you to potentially move each one toward the upper right quadrant.

FOUR MESSAGES FOR TEAM DEVELOPMENT

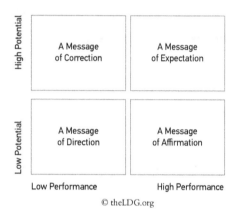

© theLDG.org

LOW PERFORMERS WITH LOW POTENTIAL. These team members need a message of *direction* to alert them to unacceptable performance.

HIGH PERFORMERS WITH LOW POTENTIAL. These team members need a message of *affirmation* to challenge them to continue performing beyond expectations.

LOW PERFORMERS WITH HIGH POTENTIAL. These team members need a message of *correction* to determine if they can improve performance.

HIGH PERFORMANCE WITH HIGH POTENTIAL. These team members need a message of *expectation* to challenge and reward their capacity in setting a new standard for best practice performance.

PERSONAL DRIVE

The original Nine Box Grid only considers performance and potential. The Leadership Development Group has added a third dimension that tells the whole story of where your direct reports land on the grid and what your development agenda is in your role as the leader-coach. This tool can provide an understanding of how to see each team member and how to develop their performance potential. Coaching conversations teach them how to do the same with their own direct reports. It is an approach to cascade leadership development throughout the culture of your company on all levels.

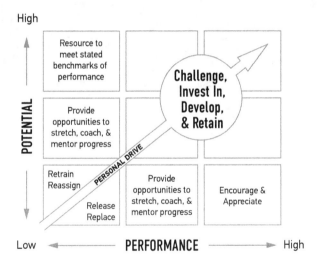

Nine Box LDG Variation © theLDG.org

THE CORE

The leadership assignment is not to level the playing field. Actually, we must all admit that the playing field isn't level. So, accept the reality that team members are at different places in each matrix and work to move everyone toward the upper right.

REFLECTION QUESTIONS: Who is in what section on each matrix? What is your coaching communication strategy for those in each box? How long will you wait to address the development of each team member?

CAPACITY MULTIPLIER #2

Organizational Enablers:
A Workplace Culture that Invests
in the Everyday Leader

◆

We believe in relentlessly refining our skills and
knowledge, as a team and as individuals.

—LIZ LIU
Head of Culture, Scopely

36

THREE AVENUES: HOW TO EXTEND LEADERSHIP CAPACITY

Growing leaders invest in their own professional development by understanding where they fall short in demonstrating character and competence. Self-discovery is gained from research-based assessments and 360-degree feedback from team members. These insights identify the behaviors and skills consistently interfering with effective practice in current roles or preventing their being considered for a future advanced role. Growing leaders weave together those observations with personal insights from three aspects of everyday life.

1. RELATIONSHIPS. Leaders committed to developing their capacity never limit their network to an existing group of relational connections. Their goal is to become more

intentional and strategic in expanding the circle of professional colleagues, including a priority of who they spend the most time with internally and externally. Every addition to your professional learning community exponentially increases your network. Who you spend time with influences who you are becoming. Who you spend time with opens up avenues of opportunity represented in that collective group.

2. EXPERIENCES. The application of new learning in stretch assignments beyond your typical work develops improved leadership habits. In the *Power of Habit: Why We Do What We Do in LIfe and Business*, Charles Duhigg introduces the reader of his bestselling book to the idea of Keystone Habits.[1] These are habits that have a chain reaction that help other good habits take hold. Keystone leadership habits have a ripple effect that strengthen the entire leadership enterprise of the individual. When is the last time you volunteered for a work assignment that challenged your current leadership habits? Stretching today's competencies expands tomorrow's capacity!

3. DISCIPLINES. Leadership addresses the consistency of how you respond to organizational challenges and opportunities. Yes, leadership is an art and a science. The science side represents the behaviors and skills critical to leading others. The artful side of the equation is knowing when to break bad habits and discover what should replace them. Are you aware of your leadership habits and patterns? Could team members articulate them? Is it time to replace bad habits with better disciplines that expand your capacity?

THE CORE

The best leaders are lifelong learners. They continue to refine the behaviors and skills needed in their current role and any anticipated roles.

REFLECTION QUESTIONS: Do you feel guilty taking time for your professional development as if you are somehow cheating the organization or not doing your job? Do you understand that increasing your competence adds value to the organization?

DELEGATION: THE URGENT AND THE MORE IMPORTANT

Delegation is one of the most overlooked skills needed in every leader's toolbox. In delegating, leaders plan how to offload tasks someone else can do so they can lead in more strategic areas. Most leaders can identify one thing they keep doing weekly that someone else could do. In saving one hour per week, the cumulative annual benefit would be more than a full work week for other important tasks. In practical terms, this leader could schedule one full day every other month to step away from operational leadership urgencies and spend time offsite addressing the more important tasks of strategic leadership.

Delegation Maximizes Capacity

Delegation is a learned competency answering the who, what, when, and how interrogatives. Leaders have three options: (1) Not delegating, (2) Delegating prematurely, or (3) Delegating developmentally. The typical excuses leaders offer of why they don't delegate:

"I need control."

"I can do it faster."

"It takes too long to train someone else."

"I can't trust anyone else with doing this task."

Leaders who maintain full control of all the details in operational work *make four damaging mistakes:*

1. THEY BECOME THE BOTTLENECK TO PRODUCTIVITY. Leaders who assume they can do it faster or better miss seeing the future productive potential represented in the entire team. When other team members learn the skills needed for new assignments, more people produce more work.

2. THEY HINDER THE DEVELOPMENT OF EMERGING LEADERS. Not delegating leads to confusion and frustration when team members are given full responsibility but not full authority. The application of new learning in stretch assignments is what contributes to increased team capacity. When delegation is done well, it solves the attraction, retention, and engagement issues of those employees.

3. THE TRICKLE UP EFFECT. If you don't delegate, then you are working below your paygrade. In other words, you are getting paid too much if you are doing work your direct reports should be doing. It happens under pressure when you default to your operational subject matter expertise. You take over work for your direct reports which results in several possibilities: (a) You have no time left over for the strategic leadership you need to be providing, (b) You are burning the candle at both ends and your work-life balance is out of whack, (c) Your boss picks up the work you are not getting to, (d) Then they aren't doing their full role while they pick up for you, and (e) the *Trickle Up Effect* takes over, and the organization misses out on it full productive potential.

4. THEY KEEP THEMSELVES BUSY IN OPERATIONS. Leaders are often subject matter experts in the tactical side of operations which is, in part, why they were promoted. In times of urgency and stress, it is their easy default to step back into operations and take control once again. It keeps them from having time to address the strategic side of leadership.

FULL RESPONSIBILITY AND HOW MUCH AUTHORITY?

What could you offload, who would you give it to, and how would you get them up to speed to take on full responsibility with full authority? The Delegation Matrix represents four different messages to team members at varying points of readiness for full responsibility and full authority of new assignments.

THE DELEGATION MATRIX

© theLDG.org

DELEGATING DEVELOPMENTALLY

Delegation is a developmental process that leverages four messages designed to meet team members at each stage of readiness to take on a new responsibility.

> » STAGE ONE. *Low Responsibility/Low Authority.* The leader communicates to the team member: "Come watch me do this." Then, they debrief on what the team member observed.

> » STAGE TWO. *High Responsibility/Low Authority.* The leader communicates: "Let's do this together. You help me." Then, they discuss what the team member observed, experienced, and learned.

> » STAGE THREE. *Low Responsibility/High Authority.* The leader says: "Let's do this together. This time, I'll watch you do it." Then, the leader provides feedback for discussion from what was observed.

> » STAGE FOUR. *High Responsibility/High Authority.* The leader says: "Now you do it, and I will be available to support you." Then, the leader delegates full responsibility and full authority with ongoing review and support.

THE CORE

Delegation is a handing off process combined with a *letting go* process. *Handing off* is an assignment the leader gives to a team member. *Letting go* gives the team member the authority to use time and organizational resources to reach a shared goal. When leaders skip any of the four steps to delegate full responsibility and full authority, it diminishes leadership capacity. The "Delegation ROI?" The team member gets a stretch assignment that expands their leadership capacity. The leader frees up time and resources to give attention to issues with greater organizational complexity. The organization expands its productive potential.

REFLECTION QUESTIONS: What do you keep doing every week that someone else on your team could do? Is it harder for you to delegate responsibility or to give full authority? If this is difficult for you, what is one small thing you could delegate tomorrow and truly let go?

38

NETWORKING: CONNECTIONS LEAD TO NEW TRANSITIONS

Maybe I was overly optimistic when I read the book, *The 100-Year Life: Living and Working in an Age of Longevity*, by Lynda Gratton and Andrew Scott from London Business School. My parents and grandparents lived well into their nineties, and my dad was still driving at ninety-six. So, the book seemed relevant! *The 100-Year Life* reviews the old model of life with three phases: grow up, work, and then retire. The dilemma in that approach is that retirement could last another thirty-five years, and what will people do during that part of life to find meaning and purpose up to the possibility of age 100. The new way being proposed is to think in terms of life as a series of transitions. In their research, Gratton and Scott suggest three characteristics of people who will be successful in making transitions throughout life: self-knowledge, diverse networks, and a mindset of openness to new experiences.[1]

Regarding their ideas of diverse networks and openness, they suggest the following on page 95 of *The 100-Year Life*: "*Since your identity is fundamentally embedded in relationships and friendships, as you begin to make a transition you inevitably begin to shift connections. You are searching for new role models and kindred spirits who are on the same transition and with whom you can begin to understand the rules of the game. As a consequence, transformation does not occur in isolation, nor does it typically occur within the same group of friends. As you make these new connections, you inevitably let go of some from the past. This is important, because the people who know you best are the very ones most likely to hinder transformation rather than help it.*"

There is a leadership lesson in these insights that applies to adult development all the way to age 100. Leadership is about continual transformation to meet the needs of growing and changing organizations. Leaders at all levels should regularly network internally and especially externally. If you don't make time to expand your connections, then it never happens. New connections stretch you in new ways and open up new doors of opportunity. It may be in another industry with its own network, their way of leading, their approach to developing as a leader, or their career best practices. The agenda is to identify a short list of people you want to meet. Start small. Connect at times and places convenient for the person you are meeting. Most importantly, come prepared with questions to ask. Do your homework about their work and their company.

Contacts Count is a consulting organization that provides business network training. They recommend two books providing practical insight: *Make Your Contacts Count,* by Anne Baber and Lynne Waymon, and *Strategic Connections: The New Face of Networking in a Collaborative*

World, by Anne Baber, Lynne Waymon, Andre Alphonso, and Jim Wylde. In the second book, the authors identify Eight Networking Competencies:

1. COMMIT TO A NETWORKER IDENTITY. Appreciate how personality and mindset affect one's ability to build relationships.

2. TAKE A STRATEGIC APPROACH. Align networking activities with organizational initiatives. Use networks to accomplish specific goals. Choose optimum venues.

3. ENVISION THE IDEAL NETWORK. Capitalize on opportunities and build network capacity.

4. DEVELOP TRUSTING RELATIONSHIPS. View relationship development in six stages and manage the trust-building process by teaching character and competence.

5. INCREASE SOCIAL ACUMEN. Be more confident and professional by mastering relationship rituals and understanding the elements of likeability.

6. ENGAGE PEOPLE. Spark rich conversation to build and sustain relationships.

7. COMMUNICATE EXPERTISE. Use examples and stories to teach contacts about organizational, team, or individual expertise, talents, experience, and interests.

8. CREATE ORGANIZATIONAL VALUE. Employ networking tools and strategies to contribute to organizational success.[2]

Want to expand your leadership capacity? Expand your network internally and externally to identify new skills for leading in new ways.

THE CORE

Networking is today's investment in tomorrow. Identify who you should be connecting with, both internally and externally. Connections lead to opportunities but also serve as a collection of subject-matter experts you can reach out to at unexpected times of trouble or professional opportunity. The resources at Contacts Count will help you be intentional and focused: www.contactscount.com

REFLECTION QUESTIONS: Who are the five people with whom you should connect within your organization to gain a better comprehensive perspective of your company? Who are the five on your list outside of your company? How will you connect? What will your agenda of questions include?

THE TIES THAT BIND: THE CONFLICT THAT DIVIDES

What is it about the leaders who pull more than push team members toward strategic outcomes? Seven connections strengthen the capacity of your team by an attraction approach more than a command and control approach.

TRUST TIED TO INTEGRITY

Trust is built slowly, and it can be demolished in a careless word or an ill-timed decision. The gradual building process of trust is based on the consistency of who you are. Does your public-self match your private-self? Integrity is built when everyone is looking and when no one is looking.

Communication Tied to Clarity and Consistency

Of all your leadership tools, communication is the most important. Clarity implies that no one is confused once you are done talking. Consistency demands that everyone hears the same message. Add to that better listening. It means asking good questions. Then be quiet and listen to understand.

Humility Tied to Reputation

Reputation is what people say about you when you are not around. Leaders who give credit and take the blame demonstrate a humility of the team's importance over the leader's reputation. Leadership is getting things done through a group of people. Invest in their success, then notice, comment, and celebrate individual contributors and team successes.

Strengths Tied to a Well-Rounded Team

We grow up with a myth early in life that convinces us to try to be the well-rounded team member. Capacity grows when team members bring their best strengths more often to the work of the team. That doesn't ignore non-strength areas but recognizes there may be ways to manage around or compensate for those areas through other team members.

Conflict Tied to Innovation

Leaders learn to reframe conflict as an expected and positive part of team life. Healthy conflict generates new ideas, innovation, and industry best practices. It is important to keep conflict between ideas not individuals. Leaders model that and manage team conflict as well.

Delegation Tied to Developmental Readiness

Leaders who struggle to delegate become the bottleneck to team development and team productivity. In addition, it keeps the leader from moving from operational leadership to strategic leadership. Delegation necessitates the readiness of team members for full responsibility and full authority and the willingness of the leader to hand off as well as let go.

Respect Tied to Interpersonal Attitudes

Respect is the gift you give to every person in the organization at every employment level. Momentary conversations take a matter of seconds but communicate your interest, and at times concern, for another person. What attitude does your behavior communicate to others?

When Conflict Divides

Over-Under Managing can create conflict between the leader and the direct report. Conflict can bring clarity to these working relationships before a valued team member ends up leaving the manager and not as often the job. Healthy conflict generates innovative thinking and best practice solutions. The question for leaders is how to keep conflict around competing ideas, not between individuals. Consider reading: *Getting to Yes: Negotiating Agreement Without Giving In* by Fisher, Ury, and Paton with publication editions in 1981, 1991, and 2011.[1] It is a classic resource on negotiation theory that aims for win-win agreements. This was developed as part of the Harvard Negotiation Project addressing negotiation and conflict resolution. This strategy unfolds in three phases: analysis of the problem, planned ways of responding, and discussion of a possible solution in which all parties can agree.

Four principles guide this approach:

1. SEPARATE PEOPLE FROM THE PROBLEM. People get personally involved from their perspective on the issue at hand and take other positions as personal attacks. Staying focused on the issue provides clarity on the root cause without damaging relationships.

2. FOCUS ON INTERESTS, NOT POSITIONS. The authors suggest, "Your position is something you have decided upon. Your interests are what caused you to so decide." (Read the context surrounding this quote on page 42 of *Getting to Yes*). Positions result in a win-lose outcome. When you define a problem in terms of interests, it's possible to find a solution that satisfies both individuals.

3. GENERATE A VARIETY OF OPTIONS BEFORE CONCLUDING AGREEMENT. Brainstorming alternatives leads to a second and separate step of evaluating those options in terms of interests.

4. GET TO AN AGREEMENT BASED ON OBJECTIVE CRITERIA. Criteria-based decisions are more objective especially when you give weight to each of the criteria. A simple calculation applying the agreed-upon criteria to every option with a ranking (low=1, medium=2, high=3) results in a numerical conclusion. This can be done in a number of ways. See Chapter 24 in *Leadership Core* where I have described three tools for effective decision making in uncertain times.

The interpersonal issues that complicate any approach to conflict resolution include bias, perception, emotions, and inadequate communicators who have a hard time listening for understanding rather than for agreement. Patrick Lencioni ties healthy conflict to a foundation of trust in his best-selling book, *The Five Dysfunctions of a Team: A Leadership Fable.*[2] David Horsager's best-seller, *The Trust*

Edge: How Top Leaders Gain Faster Results, Deepen Relationships, and a Stronger Bottom Line, addresses how to foster trust within a team and throughout an entire organization.[3] If trust is missing within your team, it is your number-one assignment to find balance between over managing or under managing your team.

.... ⵣ ....

THE CORE

The seven ties are not complicated or difficult to implement. Every connection between leader and team touches your capacity as the leader as well as the team's productive potential. Stepping into conflict and managing the flow of ideas and conclusions also adds to your capacity by multiplying the conflicting ideas that can lead to an uptick in your productive potential.

REFLECTION QUESTIONS: Which of the seven ties will most strengthen your capacity to lead more effectively and efficiently? Which one is already successful? Which of the four conflict principles will you develop as a new leadership habit?

MAKE TECHNOLOGY YOUR FRIEND: THE AI LEADER

Technology can be your friend, your obsession, or your worst nightmare. Chances are, you've experienced all three! My advice is to see technology as a tool. Learn to use the tool. Don't be used by the tool. I am not personally wired for technological expertise, but I can't deny that digital transformation is defining the future of how work is getting done. Michael M. Lombardo and Robert W. Eichinger include a chapter called "Technical Learning" in their book, *FYI: For Your Improvement, A Guide for Development and Coaching*. The competency profile describes those of us who are unskilled in this area of leadership:

> » Doesn't learn new technical skills readily

» Is among the last to learn or adopt new technology

» May be stuck on past technologies and resist switching to new ones

» May be intimidated by new technology

» May lack experience or exposure to new technology

» May not be interested in things technical or areas involving lots of detail

» May not know how to or may reject using others to learn new technologies

» May have a fear of doing something wrong that will cause harm or bring embarrassment[1]

Needless to say, I can identify with each of these statements. The world of technology is changing daily, and the competition is pushing every leader to become conversant with the technical language of the day. The following words are connected but are not synonymous with each other:

TECHNOLOGY is scientific knowledge that we put into practice to solve common problems to make life better for all of us. The solution may be the invention of useful tools or services that improve human life in specific ways, such as patient healthcare or making all forms of transportation more safe and more efficient.

DIGITAL TECHNOLOGY processes and stores data by converting information (words, pictures, or sounds) into numbers or digits. This is a binary code represented as a combination of 0's and 1's. Digital transformation, like going paperless, is the use of digital technology to create more efficient business processes or to improve the customer experience. For example, Chatbot is a computer program that answers a caller's simple question using natural language rather than waiting for someone to answer a call. Cloud computing is an example of digital technology that leverages remote hardware and software as services which can be scaled up or down as needed through a subscription-based model. Storing and sharing content associated with an individual or enterprise on Cloud infrastructure is just one of many possibilities.

ARTIFICIAL INTELLIGENCE (AI) is the intelligence demonstrated by machines. The intent of AI is to create technology that allows computers or other kinds of machines to simulate collective human intelligence. The safety features of driver assistance technology like lane departure warning systems and self-driving cars are examples.

MIT and the Sloan School of Management's Initiative on the Digital Economy are among the global thought leaders tackling these interrelated topics and the impact of digital technology on businesses, the economy, and society at large. Gerald Kane wrote an article in the MIT Sloan School of Management Review dated July 9, 2018, called "Common Traits of the Best Digital Leaders."[2] The premise of Kane's article is that "leaders must develop new skills to effectively guide their organizations into the uncertain future of the digital age." Kane suggests four actions to describe leadership literacy for those who understand the new digital world in which business functions:

1. THEY PROVIDE VISION AND PURPOSE. They have a strong vision of where they are going and opportunities to execute the vision.

2. THEY CREATE CONDITIONS FOR EXPERIMENTATION. They foster curiosity with risk-tolerant employees as they face their biggest challenges.

3. THEY EMPOWER PEOPLE TO THINK DIFFERENTLY. They see what is possible as well as what customers expect in

terms of cost value, experience value, and platform value.

4. THEY ENABLE COLLABORATION ACROSS BOUNDARIES. They work through the obstacles of culture, mindset, and silo thinking. Digital transformation demands collaboration beyond internal communication.

The invitation for leaders who are averse to technology is to decide that it is beyond valuable for them to engage with new technology. Begin by seeking out people and resources who will help you understand the things you need to learn. Know what technologies perform what types of tasks. Know the potential and the limitations of each. Know enough so you don't waste organizational resources on the wrong technology for the work that needs to be done. Do your homework to know which vendors provide systems that can be implemented quickly. Surround yourself with other knowledgeable people whom you trust. Lastly, don't feel guilty if this is a weakness for you. At the same time, don't hide your lack of knowledge. Many people of all ages need help in this area! Thomas Edison said it well, "Just because something doesn't do what you planned it to do doesn't mean it's useless."

THE CORE

One of the smarter leadership moves you can make is to share the digital learning curve with your executive team. Make digital literacy part of your executive leadership team agenda by having each member lead a specific digital discussion. Perhaps rotate through some aspect of this topic until everyone in the board room feels ownership. Learn together so you can discuss it intelligently and make wise decisions.

REFLECTION QUESTIONS: Do you know what you don't yet know? That's conscious incompetence which is better than unconscious incompetence. Where should you begin?

41

HARDWIRING NEW LEADERSHIP HABITS: THINK, TALK, ACT, REFLECT

Capacity grows when new leadership behaviors and leadership competencies are hardwired and form new habits. Leadership development begins with the assumption that people can change, but one's development potential is limited by organizational support, developmental resources, and personal drive. How do you know development is working? It's not an easy question to answer in a way that will satisfy those who allocate the funds to continue this work. In the end, transformation is demonstrated in your consistency of improved leadership habits in the way you think, talk, and act. Hardwiring incremental change in new habits of leadership practice starts with what you are thinking about. Conversations with subject matter experts, colleagues, or an executive coach reinforces new learning by adding the perspective of others to enrich your understanding and application. The evidence of greater competence in a specific skill area of leadership is finally demonstrated in the consistency of more productive leadership behaviors. You grow as a leader by taking small steps that stretch you in new incremental ways.

THE THINK, TALK, ACT, REFLECT MODEL©

Leadership capacity is the potential to lead in more complex organizational roles. Addressing a leadership competency gap represents the tactical work that results in increased capacity. A career-long commitment to professional growth and development maximizes your leadership capacity. Thoughts lead to words, and words lead to actions. Consider the Think, Talk, Act, Reflect model from The Leadership Development Group:

STEPPING STONE #1 - THINK. What do you need to know about a specific leadership behavior or competency to understand its significance and its application in your current or anticipated leadership role? How is someone skilled or unskilled in this area described? The current research on competency transformation suggests micro learning with on-the-job application in stretch assignments. Learning is incremental and so is development.

STEPPING STONE #2 - TALK. Is there a colleague you can connect with in a one-on-one conversation, or is there an informal professional learning community of like-minded leaders you could join? An executive coach can focus on the application of learning with scenario planning customized to your workplace reality.

Discussion enhances the value of your learning and provides new perspectives on its application.

STEPPING STONE #3 – ACT. Application is what transforms. Trial and error are part of learning new attitudes, words, and behaviors that demonstrate positive influence (character) and effective action (competence) as a leader. Are you willing to stretch yourself in new ways of leading?

STEPPING STONE #4 – REFLECT. Structured review and discussion of learnings from trial and error lead to another cycle of learning, valuing, applying, and reviewing in incremental steps for each iteration of growth.

HARDWIRING LEADERSHIP CHARACTER AND LEADERSHIP COMPETENCE WORKSHEET

Leadership Development Processes	Defining Questions	Goal	Character or Competence:		
Think 10%	What do I need to learn about this character quality or leadership competency?	Identify the primary sources to increase incremental change (How will you learn more about it?)			
Talk 20%	With whom can I discuss my new learning: a colleague or executive coach?	Discuss your new learning and how it applies in specific scenarios in your leadership.			
Act 50%	How, where and when will I apply what I am learning?	1) Make it a stretch assignment. 2) Start small.			
Reflect 20%	How do I know I am improving my positive influence (character) or effective action (competence)	Use the *Ask Daily Questions* Reflection Exercise for 21 workdays. See: *Afterword*			

© www.theLDG.org

THE CORE

Most have a personal default in preferring one of four
approaches to adult learning styles. A holistic approach
incorporates all of these steps to let new ways of leading
become internalized in a way that expands our leadership
capacity. This is when change, growth, and development have
the potential to help us achieve our full productive potential.

REFLECTION QUESTIONS: What are you thinking about
and learning as a result? What are you talking about and then
understanding more? What stretch assignments are you tackling
that apply new learning? How are you debriefing what went well
and what didn't? Will you consider using the *Hardwiring Leadership
Behaviors and Leadership Competencies Worksheet* to create your plan to
extend your leadership capacity?

42

GUARDRAILS: KEEPING LEADERS ON TRACK

Leadership is never about being liked, at least it shouldn't be. It is about being respected while you are also respectful of others. Eight questions will help you focus on the right things, at the right time, in the right way, for the right reasons, and with the right people. In other words, get it right! That is leadership capacity at its best.

YOUR LEADERSHIP FINAL EXAM

1. Are you a step ahead or a step behind your **competition**? Are you following them, or are they following you? Might you need to swallow pride and collaboratively follow each other?

2. Do you design your own **best practices** through a continual process of incremental tests of change? Or, do you just accept industry best practices that fit another context but may not be uniquely applicable to your organization?

3. Do you know the limits of your leadership **capacity**? Do you know how to manage capacity limits? Are you willing to address character or competence gaps to enhance your leadership capacity?

4. Do you know the signs of when a key team member is becoming **divisive** in undermining your leadership? The signs include someone: spreading rumors, triangulating other team members against you, becoming more aloof, using humor that is actually criticism, showing lack of engagement, or avoids looking at you in the eye. Too many leaders make the mistake of waiting too long to deal directly with a toxic team member. When you wait, it costs more in team engagement and productivity. What is the prospect of turning them into an engaged and satisfied team member? If that is not likely, then what will you do? When?

5. Can you say, "I don't know?" Can you say, "I'm sorry?" Can you say, "**I was wrong?**" Sustainable leaders are willing to say all these things.

6. Do you know the cost of justifying your **executive rudeness** in the name of importance and busyness? It happens when you walk by others while attending to more important things on your cell phone. The "Nobodys" are always "Somebodys." Their perception of your leadership is their reality of who you are as a person.

7. Do you **give credit**. How often do you catch someone doing something right and tell them? Do you recognize, reward, and celebrate teams and team members? When is the last time you did this, apart from the year-end holiday party?

8. Are you breaking through **organizational silos** by aligning teams to shared outcomes with cross-functional strategies?

THE CORE

Organizations benefit from leaders who are in it for the long haul. The resilience of sustainable leadership is about the ability to adapt to change long before it is too late. It's about leaders who are agile enough to adjust their leadership competency mix in order to transform the organizational culture. It's an important but lofty goal to achieve strategic outcomes while consistently modeling corporate values. It's about the connection of character and competence as you push the limits of your capacity as a leader. It's never too late nor impossible to make changes. Just start with one of the troubling questions above. Start small. Just start.

REFLECTION QUESTIONS: Is your largest effectiveness gap in the area of leadership character or leadership competence? Have you ever tested your capacity through stretch assignments that invite you to close existing gaps between what is and what should be?

Resilient optimism is the core of leadership capacity.

RESILIENCE: LEADING FOR THE LONG HAUL

◆

RESILIENCE: LEADING FOR THE LONG HAUL

Every leader will face at least one impossible situation during their leadership tenure. That time is described as having your back against the wall, with no way out, completely alone, and the feeling of gloom you have when it seems like the end is near. Consider Mark Watney, the astronaut on a manned mission to Mars in the movie version of Andy Weir's novel. If you haven't seen the movie, Mark, played by Matt Damon, is presumed dead after an incredible storm on the surface of Mars. He is left behind by his crew in their attempt to escape disaster. In the 20th Century Fox movie, *The Martian*, Matt Damon as Mark Watney demonstrates the leadership quality of resilience through his survival strategies.[1] If you are interested in how it all turns out, then I will let you watch the movie! The insights for leadership from *The Martian* follow below.

LEADERSHIP SURVIVAL STRATEGIES

Surviving the impossible requires every resource that sustaining leaders can access. Consider six survival strategies.

CORE VALUES. Those resilient enough for sustainability in leadership for the long haul find their grounding in personal values that they believe as ideas but live as behaviors. Angela Armstrong, PhD, said it this way: "I define resilience as the ability to take the challenges and changes of life in your stride and say yes to the opportunities that excite you. Core values are the principles or belief that you view as being of central importance and that serve to dictate your behavior and actions."

GIVING UP. It is a mindset that sustaining leaders never ever succumb to. It's the easiest way out, but that is not what great leaders choose.

ONE STEP. In the midst of the impossible, a leader is rarely able to look at a strategic sequence from today's brutal realities to tomorrow's final solution. The focus can only be on the next step that seems apparent and might very well lead to other avenues of resolution.

LIMITED RESOURCES. This is not a time to deal in the "if only" thoughts about what would be needed for ideal circumstances. It is rarely ideal, so effective leaders clarify and classify every possible resource that is actually within reach.

COUNTERINTUITIVE THINKING. Concluding that you are bound by intuitive ideas keeps you from getting outside the boundaries of current limitations. A sustaining leader will connect

the dots among all resources available to create an uncanny
assortment of possibilities.

ACCESS EXPERTS. The chance of direct connection to subject-
matter experts may be improbable but not impossible. Wise use of
social media resources will help with your network and might give
you a mosaic of connections you never thought possible.

LEARNED OPTIMISM

These leadership survival strategies distinguish pessimists from
optimists. Pessimists explain life events as if bad things are always
bound to happen and the negative results last forever. Optimists live
with confident expectation that good things will happen to them
in spite of life's difficulties. It's more than a mentality because the
optimism literally has the power to change the outcome. When the
bad times come, the optimistic leader doesn't give up. They aren't
the victim. They see the trouble as a challenge to be overcome.
Optimism leads to better physical and mental health, longer life,
lower stress, higher motivation and performance, and career success.
An optimistic view builds resilience so you can bounce back after
setbacks.

Martin E.P. Seligman is the founding father of Positive Psychology
and introduced the world to the idea of *Learned Optimism*. It's
the opposite of *Learned Helplessness* when people believe they are
incapable of changing their circumstances when experiencing a
stressful event. In his book Seligman suggests that setbacks are an
unending life experience for pessimists, but optimists see setbacks
as new insights into how to live more effectively. He seems to
understand the reality of failure in life but sees the difference in the
reaction between resilient people and pessimistic people. The resilient
have found a way to challenge negative self-talk. For more insight
into Seligman's discussion, see his book, *Learned Optimism: How to
Change Your Mind and Your Life*.[2]

THE CORE

Creative staying power increases the odds of making the impossible possible. It will demand every ounce of leadership skill, personal determination, innovative resourcefulness, collaborative effort, emotional intelligence, and physical stamina. Is there always a way home and back to normal? Honestly, No. Yet, sustaining leaders will always see an inevitable ending as a new beginning.

REFLECTION QUESTIONS: Where do you fall on the optimism/pessimism spectrum? What is one leadership shortcoming that you need to address to be a better leader? Is it an aspect of character that is tied to positive influence? Is it an area of competence needed in your next steps forward that will contribute to your effective action? When will you do something about it?

AFTERWORD

◆

DON'T JUST DO SOMETHING, SIT THERE

On one memorable summer day, I read a blog post by Marshall Goldsmith titled, "6 Questions That Will Set You Up to Be Super Successful." [1] Goldsmith's articles are always a global experience depending on where he is when he writes! This time, he shared a daily reflection exercise that he personally does at the end of every day. He works with six questions he has identified as primary areas of growth and development. He scores himself on a simple one to five scale for each question, then he exchanges his numbers with a colleague. I liked the concept and started to do it myself. For twenty-one days, I tracked my progress on priorities in life. It was an amazing journey.

For the first two weeks, it was somewhat mechanical. "Oh, that's right, I need to score my six questions before I can go leave the office," I would say. By day seventeen, I realized that I was not satisfied with some scores in two or three areas. I decided to be more aware of those as I went through my day rather than just reflect at the end of the day. That's when the magic happened. Now those questions were informing my day and prompting some new habits in how I navigate the people and projects of the day.

I have included a copy below of my version of the *Twenty-One Day Goldsmith Reflection Exercise*. I am sharing it with Goldsmith's permission, but please check out his writing on this and other topics as well. My encouragement to you is that you start by identifying your own six questions. Then at the end of each day just reflect on how well you did in each area. This is one of the best coaching tools I have found to reinforce new habit choices with self-accountability. Consider how you might use it to:

1. Shape leadership CHARACTER that leads to positive influence in those you lead.

2. Build leadership COMPETENCE that leads to effective action with those you lead.

3. Stretch leadership CAPACITY that leads to maximizing potential in those you lead.

Those three statements are the thesis of *Leadership Core*. Give attention to your character, competence, and capacity as a leader and the culture and climate of your workplace will be transformed! Perhaps some of what we are accomplishing at work will carry over to our homes and improve relationships with those we love and live with every day. And just maybe, it can move from job to home to our communities and one day it could even change the world. One leader at a time. One team member at a time. One department… one division…one company at a time. Character plus competence extends your capacity to be more effective in every part of your life!

Respectfully,

Dr. D…

ASK DAILY QUESTIONS
THE GOLDSMITH REFLECTION EXERCISE

"What if you could implement a process that costs almost nothing, takes about three minutes a day, and if you stick with it, will help you achieve your full potential? Would you try it out?"

"The challenge is to ask Active questions rather than Passive questions which changes the focus of your answers and empowers you to make changes you would not otherwise consider."

"There is a hug difference between 'Do you have clear goals?' and 'Did you do your best to set clear goals for yourself.' The former is trying to determine the individual's state of mind, and the latter challenges the individual to describe and defend a course of action."

Adapted from Marshall Goldsmiths blog.
His Reflective Exercise is more focused on action than the state of mind.

Goldsmith's six active questions include:

1. Did I do my best to increase my happiness?
2. Did I do my best to find meaning?
3. Did I do my best to be engaged?
4. Did I do my best to build positive relationships?
5. Did I do my best to set clear goals?
6. Did I do my best to make progress toward goal achievement?

Asking Your Daily Reflection Questions

Habits take twenty-one days to build into your life, so use the *Goldsmith Reflection Exercise* for three weeks. Find a friend or colleague who will do this activity with you at the end of every day...each using your own list of six questions. Share your numerical rating for your questions each day. The accountability is invaluable if you want to improve your leadership effectiveness and job satisfaction.

My three focus areas for development coaching include:

_____
_____
_____

The Six Development Questions for Daily Reflection:

1. Did I do my best to
2. Did I do my best to
3. Did I do my best to
4. Did I do my best to
5. Did I do my best to
6. Did I do my best to

Use a five point scale to rate each of your daily questions regarding your EQ competencies:
1=Very Dissatisfied **2**=Dissatisfied **3**=Neither **4**=Satisfied **5**=Very Satisfied

LEADERSHIP CORE

Leadership Character + Leadership Competence =
Leadership Capacity

Or translated this way...

Positive Influence + Effective Action =
Leadership Potential

The Character Competence Capacity Matrix

© theLDG.org

THE CORE
& REFLECTION
QUESTIONS

⋯⋯⋯⋯⋯⋯⋯⋯⋯⋯⋯⋯⋯⋯⋯ ◆ ⋯⋯⋯⋯⋯⋯⋯⋯⋯⋯⋯⋯⋯⋯⋯

When leaders develop their character alongside developing their competency, it enhances their overall leadership capacity. That is when people will trust you, and trust is the essential ingredient in leadership influence. It speaks to our ability and readiness to lead at higher levels of organizational complexity. The numbering below corresponds with the chapter numbers throughout the book.

CHAPTER 1

THE JOHARI WINDOW 360: BLIND SPOTS: Blind Spots get in the way of your leadership effectiveness and efficiency, and the only way to identify them is to ask others for feedback. Leaders who have the courage to be vulnerable by asking, listening, and responding are investing in the ongoing development of leadership character that leads to positive influence in work relationships.

REFLECTION QUESTIONS: Who will you ask to give you honest feedback about your Blind Spots? When?

CHAPTER 2

The Leader's Reputation: When Integrity Isn't Easy: Emotionally smart leaders will generally outplay their IQ in much of life. IQ may get you a job, but EQ will create sustainability for the long haul. Owning and managing your emotional responses to troubling situations and people is at the heart of leadership character and your integrity in the eyes of others. It either advances your influence or negates that half of the leadership formula: Positive Influence + Effective Action = Leadership Capacity.

REFLECTION QUESTIONS: Which area do you need to develop further: feeling your emotions or dealing with your emotions? What situations or people trigger intense emotions at work?

CHAPTER 3

HUMBLY SPEAKING: WHO'S THE HERO: How do you see yourself? How do you see your team? Would those closest to you say that you are a person of character who consistently displays an attitude of humility? Humility isn't a weakness when it is genuine. Confidence won't become arrogance when you take time to understand the points of view from those around you.

REFLECTION QUESTIONS: On a continuum from 1 to 10, what are you like? 1 = Humble. 10 = Arrogant. What is one thing you could do that will help you move toward greater humility?

CHAPTER 4

FAILURE: WHERE CHARACTER IS FORGED: Four lessons can be learned from failure: (1) Create a team culture where failure is expected and allowed as part of the journey to success. (2) Provide a pathway for failure recovery. (3) Discuss the failure with the team or team member. Ask the first "why" of what is behind the failure. Then ask why once again (and again and again) in order to explore cause and effect relationships that underlie what happened. (4) Identify the insights that will help you build on the failure as a step toward success and avoid repeating the same mistake another time. Learning from your failure builds integrity and character in how you see yourself and how others see you.

REFLECTION QUESTION: What was the biggest failure that kept you from a new beginning?

CHAPTER 5

IDENTITY OR REPUTATION: LEADERS WHO CAN BE TRUSTED. Reputation is not about identity or your self-understanding. It has to do with perception of how others see you. People make observations of you and quickly conclude if they like you and if they respect you. They base the conclusion on how you look and how you sound. It may not be fair, but it is reality. Liking you is all about the interpersonal chemistry and common ground. Respecting you is the recognition of your competence in the work being done. Integrity is reinforced when liking you and respecting are aligned in the perception of others. That is when people will trust you, and trust is an essential ingredient in leadership influence.

REFLECTION QUESTIONS: What do you feel gets in the way of an accurate perception of who you really are? Are people getting an accurate reflection of your character in how you look and how you sound?

CHAPTER 6

OWN YOUR ETHICAL CODE: THE POWER OF ADVANCED DECISION MAKING. Knowing your values ahead of time will empower you when faced with an ethical situation where the right answer is not clear. Use a structured process to work through a reasoned sequence of steps that will lead to the greatest good and the least harm to the most people. Values and ethical choices are the calling card of integrity for leaders of positive character.

REFLECTION QUESTIONS: If you could rewind and work though an ethical dilemma from an earlier day, what would you do differently? How would it have changed the final decision and outcome?

CHAPTER 7

THE HIDDEN PRICE OF LEADING: THE CALLING AND THE COST. Leadership is never about a legacy of popularity. Leadership is about integrity and character. The effort to appease all critics rarely pays off in getting to the goal in a way that everyone is eager to celebrate. Sustaining leaders are willing and able to pay the price of knowing that not everyone will like them or agree with their pathway to success. Popularity will be expressed at your retirement party because people have observed the consistency of your humility, determination, sacrifice, and results. The consistency of your character will empower you to benefit from but also withstand the critics.

REFLECTION QUESTIONS: Do you want people to recall your accomplishments or recognize and respect your values at your funeral? Do you lead in such a way that people know and respect your values?

CHAPTER 8

A CIVIL WORKPLACE: TEN CULTURE-CLIMATE QUESTIONS. Leaders shape culture (the ideal). Team members determine climate (the real). How big is the gap in your organization? In your department? In your team? In you? As leaders, it is easy to overestimate the narrowness of the gap. Climate is affected by an ineffective leader or a toxic team member. Use the *Ten Culture-Climate Questions* and discuss each one with your executive team. Better yet, use a confidential online survey tool to get a cross-section of responses on these questions from every employment level in your organization. Then strategize how to close the gap that varies by department, leader, team, and team member.

REFLECTION QUESTIONS: Which of the *Ten Culture-Climate Questions* is the most troubling? Which one is most important in your development of greater character and positive influence?

CHAPTER 9

AN ENVIRONMENT OF KINDNESS: Cinderella's Code: Character is not that complicated when you narrow the discussion of respect down to two ideas. At the end of every day, ask yourself how you are doing with the fairytale values: Courage and Kindness.

REFLECTION QUESTIONS: When have you led courageously? When have you led with kindness? When was kindness missing in a leadership moment? How will you lead tomorrow in light of what you realized today?

CHAPTER 10

HIERARCHICAL ELITISM: WHEN LEADERS DON'T MODEL THE WAY. Leadership is as much about the soft skills of positive influence as the hard skills of effective action. The further up the hierarchy, the more you may want to justify the lack of interpersonal savvy because you are rewarded for working on strategy and key outcomes. If you want to develop a pipeline of emerging leaders for the next chapter of your organization, then learn to master the interpersonal competencies that support the journey from the top tier of the organization to the bottom line.

REFLECTION QUESTIONS: Can you identify someone you've been treating as less important than you? People of character work to level the social playing field and flatten any unhealthy hierarchy. Are you working on either?

CHAPTER 11

HOW TO SHUT UP: WHEN LEADERS TALK MORE THAN EVERYONE ELSE. Asking and then listening are the best indicators of respect. Asking great questions will not happen without preparation. It's actually hard work to ask thoughtful questions. If you are not a good Asker, consider books such as, *Questions That Work* by Andrew Finlayson. Then apply my 24-25-51 Rule of Communication: *Talk* 24% of the time and have something to say that team members need to hear. *Ask* 25% of the time by formulating thought provoking questions. *Listen* 51% of the time. That's over half on purpose! That might be your biggest challenge of leading.

REFLECTION QUESTIONS: Which part of the 24-25-51 Rule of Communication is the hardest for you? Having something to say that team members need to hear? Asking thought provoking questions? Listening for understanding without interrupting? Be a leader who demonstrates character in your respect of others.

CHAPTER 12

BLINDSIDED: THE TOXIC TEAM MEMBER. Never hesitate to confront the critic and explore their motives, but understand it is important to do so face to face and in a private meeting but with an objective third party present. Divisiveness is infectious, so these are important things to address. Invite them to get on board. When their attitude, words, and actions continue, the leadership mistake, admitted by many, is waiting too long to confront, learn from, reassign, retrain, or release and replace them.

REFLECTION QUESTIONS: Can you recall the first time you were blindsided by a critic? How long did you carry the emotion from that moment? Are you still recalling it? Can you still feel it? It's time to forgive them, forget it, and move on. Where are you at with this today? Is it getting easier?

CHAPTER 13

GRATITUDE: WHAT YOU SAY AND HOW TO SAY IT. Developing a culture of gratitude will have a profound impact on your team and the entire company. The assignment includes employees, customers, vendors, and investors. Find regular opportunities to catch people doing something right. Then say, *Thank You!* Those eight letters express a gratitude that drives commitment, engagement, productivity, retention, and attraction of new talent. They demonstrate respect for others by a leader of interpersonal character.

REFLECTION QUESTION: To whom can you say *Thank You* today? Say it creatively. Say it publicly when appropriate. Say it meaningfully. Put it in writing. Say it today, and don't stop all year long.

CHAPTER 14

VULNERABILITY: WHAT HAPPENS WHEN YOU ASK. Leaders of character are humble enough to admit they make mistakes in attitudes, words, and actions. Pride gets in the way of humility which gets in the way of character.

REFLECTION QUESTIONS: With whom do you need to meet first? When? How will you go about checking in with everyone on your team?

CHAPTER 15

HOW TO LEAD IN ONE WORD: IT'S A GIFT. Is leadership just one of the many things you do, or is it everything you are and do? What is the Diligence Quotient in your leadership? What will you do this week to demonstrate the careful attention and persistent work of leading others?

REFLECTION QUESTIONS: How diligent are you? On a 1 to 10 scale (10 is high) how would you rate your intentionality in the areas of: Passion, Experience, Intentionality, and ROI? How would you rate your overall intentionality to be a diligent leader?

CHAPTER 16

LEADERS SEE AROUND THE CORNER: WHAT'S NEXT? Don't forget: Strategy is the noun. Strategic is the adjective. Strategic leadership never moves forward with 100% certainty as to the destination or the route to get there. Your leadership calling is to see what others do not yet see. The collaborative invitation is to find the best way to get there. Strategic Leaders determine the pathway with their teams fully engaged in the considerations, discussions, and final decisions, while never feeling afraid to be the voice that initiates, clarifies, and leads to consensus, or to leader-initiated conclusions.

REFLECTION QUESTIONS: Who could lead each of three work teams: Assessment, Future State, and Change? Participation creates early ownership and buy-in. Do you conclude that this work needs to be ongoing with a formal annual check-in with your executive team to answer the basic questions: Where are we? Where are we going?

CHAPTER 17

LEADERS INITIATE CONTINUAL CHANGE: UNAVOIDABLE REALITIES. As leaders do the work of strategy, they compare where the company is today with where it needs to be at some predetermined time in the future. They are looking at the relevant data to see what others don't yet see. They may conclude Marshall Goldsmith's famous quote and book by this title: "What got you here won't get you there." That leads to change planning, change execution, and change transition management. People have different rates of adoption, so managing all of this is key to success.

REFLECTION QUESTIONS: Is every employee part of your process improvement initiative? What is your means of collecting ideas from all levels of employment? Are people expected to suggest improvement ideas for greater efficiency and productivity? Who leads the review and consideration of the ideas suggested? Do you report out to your organization on changes that result from ideas they suggested? Do you acknowledge whomever suggested an idea or do you acknowledge the idea but keep the person anonymous?

CHAPTER 18

LEADERSHIP AGILITY: IN TIMES OF TRANSITION. Are you willing to adjust your leadership competency profile to more effectively and efficiently meet the challenges of where your company will be if you get to that preferred future?

REFLECTION QUESTIONS: Which area of your leadership needs your immediate attention: What, How, or Why? How often do you revisit the "why" to remind every team member that what they do is important?

CHAPTER 19

YOUR PERSONAL COMMUNICATION AUDIT: SIX REFLECTIVE QUESTIONS. Communication is the primary competence of a leader. Just because something was said does not mean it was heard, understood, or agreed with. As you get to know your team and key stakeholders, the development of this core competence implies that you adapt your communication strategy to the uniqueness of each listener or group of listeners.

REFLECTION QUESTIONS: Which of the six aspects of communication is your greatest strength compared to the other five? Which one do you stumble over most often? What will you do to enhance these tools in your leadership toolbox?

CHAPTER 20

HIRING THE BEST: THREE INTERVIEW QUESTIONS. Hiring the best is very hard work. Today's employment opportunities create a challenge in attracting and retaining the best employees. Know when you need to wait and keep looking.

REFLECTION QUESTIONS: In considering the three hiring questions, who on your team would you not hire today? Why? Which of the three hiring decision questions is the most important? What percentage of hires do you prefer to be internal rather than external? What can you learn from past hiring decisions?

CHAPTER 21

BUILDING A LEADERSHIP DEVELOPMENT CULTURE:
THE ABCS. Review each of these interrogatives with your senior
leadership to honestly determine your organizational realities, both
positive and negative. Decide what you need to change, keep, or add
to your process.

REFLECTION QUESTIONS: How ready is your company
to identify potential internal candidates for succession planning?
Which of the six interrogative questions is yet unanswered? Is your
leadership development process lacking? What is one thing you can
do to move toward creating a sustainable plan?

CHAPTER 22

THE LEADER-COACH: INVEST IN EMERGING LEADERS.
Organizations that value and invest in leadership development at
every level extend the invitation to each leader to come alongside
team members and be the advocate in their development. Whatever
you model for them, they are more likely to model the same with
those they manage. Whatever you neglect in your busyness, anticipate
that they may also neglect when they are busy. The commitment
to leading as coach cascades from the top to the bottom of your
organization.

REFLECTION QUESTIONS: Which of the five Search Institute
categories is most often neglected by you? Within that category,
which actions will you begin to model with your direct reports to
practice your value and your investment in developing your team?

CHAPTER 23

OVER AND UNDER STYLES OF MANAGING: KNOWING YOUR TEAM. The leader as coach will take time to discover the capability of each team member. Managing people as part of your leadership is a delicate dance between two extremes: overmanaging or undermanaging. Each direct report needs a different compromise between the two extremes. Know your people. Know when to step in. Know when to back away. Know when to let them fail. Know how to help them learn from failure as part of their development. The goal is leveraging micro learning with macro application to achieve incremental development.

REFLECTION QUESTIONS: Do you know your team well enough to know who needs the pat on the back and who needs the kick in the pants at any given moment in their work. Do you know when to reward successful benchmark achievement or to prompt the actions that will lead to success? Catching people doing the right things is a leadership practice. Catching people missing the mark is a leadership discipline.

CHAPTER 24

DECIDING AS A TEAM: IN TIMES OF UNCERTAINTY. Three resources are available for more comprehensive and objective decision making: The Ladder of Inference, The Decision Matrix, and Team Decision Making. The Ladder of Inference is a mindset you bring into decision making moments. The Decision Matrix is the process you can use in light of that mindset. Involving your team is a way to create ownership and buy-in of the final decision.

REFLECTION QUESTION: If you could rewind your last major decision, would these tools have changed the outcome of what you decided?

CHAPTER 25

THE ORGANIZATIONAL BLUEPRINT: SEVEN BUILDING BLOCKS AND SEVEN RULES. Mission, Vision, and Values rarely, if ever, will change. Strategy, Structure, Staffing, and Systems will continue to change as the organization re-invents itself in response to a constantly changing business climate. Revisit the "Why" every thirty days as it will inevitably get fuzzy in the minds of your average team members. Being reminded of the "Why" makes continual change less traumatic for those same individuals.

REFLECTION QUESTION: Which of the seven rules need your review or revision in connecting to what preceded and what follows?

CHAPTER 26

ALLOCATING LIMITED RESOURCES: STRATEGY AND STRATEGIC. It's as simple as this: Strategy is the noun. Strategic is the adjective. Always be intentional with how you use and spend your resources.

REFLECTION QUESTIONS: Do you know the actual realities of where you are today? How broadly (externally) and how deeply (internally) are you listening in order to determine that reality? Do you have informed clarity on the final destination of your preferred future? How will you involve all team members to determine the strategy to move from here to there? Will you do whatever is required to sustain the vision, mission, and especially the values that define organizational culture while executing your strategy?

CHAPTER 27

A MEETING RHYTHM: COMMUNICATING WITH

CLARITY AND CONSISTENCY. Use your meeting rhythm to keep asking and answering these core questions. Start by letting your team weigh in on the kinds of meetings most needed to reach your shared goals.

REFLECTION QUESTIONS: The Context Question: What did we used to do? The Reality Question: What are we doing today? The Change Question: What should we do differently? The Priority Question: What should we do next? The Letting Go Question: What should we stop doing?

CHAPTER 28

LEADING IN A CRISIS: WHEN EVERYTHING GOES WRONG. Plan now for your next crisis. What do you know about crisis situations? What will you wish you had addressed before the immediate reality? Who will be on your crisis management team? What values will guide your crisis decisions?

REFLECTION QUESTIONS: What are the brutal facts of that new reality? How is it affecting your employees, customers, vendors, and investors? Are you asking each stakeholder group or just assuming? What needs to change in how you will get work done? What resources are needed to make those changes? How will you lead differently to sustain your market share? How can you outpace your competition because of your agility? How are you ranking your To Do list? What is the next step you will take?

CHAPTER 29

STARTING POINT: CALLING, CAPACITY, DEVELOPMENT. The starting point is a recognition that you often find yourself in leading positions by your initiative or by the request of others. When there is a sense of fulfillment, you may be motivated to learn how to lead more effectively and efficiently.

REFLECTION QUESTIONS: Do you have what is required for success in a new assignment? Do you have the time, resources, and ability to close the competency gap in your leadership growth agenda in light of what will be needed in this new challenge? Can you recruit and align others who will fill in those gaps? What is the career significance if you succeed? Is there a cost of failure to the company or to you professionally? Should you pass on this opportunity and wait for a better fit? Do you feel compelled to increase your leadership capacity?

CHAPTER 30

EXECUTIVE PRESENCE: IT'S ALL ABOUT PERCEPTIONS. Change the perception and change the reputation. Change the reputation and change the influence. Executive presence is how others perceive you. How you show up and how you sound are the initial criteria used by others. Eventually, the perception is defined by the balance of how much people like you and how much they respect you. Err on one side or the other and it damages your reputation. They work hand in hand. A starting place is your ability to ask great questions. It can be as simple as asking, "What do I need to know from you today?" Asking powerful questions is hard work because it takes preparation. Start with Andrew Finlayson's *Questions That Work*. It's an entire book of questions for various work situations.

REFLECTION QUESTIONS: Do you have the ability to present yourself displaying a self-confidence that you can handle uncertain times and take charge of difficult and unpredictable challenges? Can you make daunting decisions in a short time with incomplete information? Can you stand firm in conversations with your executive peers?

CHAPTER 31

DUE DILIGENCE: DO YOUR HOMEWORK. Organizations are always changing in response to the market, the competition, and the technology. Sustaining leaders anticipate those changes, communicate the reason behind the changes, and lead individuals and teams to manage the transition that follows each change event. The more you know about yourself, your team members, and your organization, the more effective you will be in your efforts to revisit and revise the strategy to successfully fulfill your mission, vision, and values.

REFLECTION QUESTIONS: When is the last time you evaluated the alignment among your mission, vision, values, strategy, structure, staffing, and systems? Will you commit to dedicating time in the near future for this important exercise?

CHAPTER 32

AN UNEXPECTED GIFT: FORGIVENESS. So, what leadership mistake do you keep stumbling over? Why is it so hard for you to accept the same forgiveness you offer to others? An executive coach may help you find your way through this, but more realistically, you may want to invest your time with a professional who can help you get to the root causes that shed light in a way to help you move forward with a freedom not otherwise possible.

REFLECTION QUESTIONS: Failure can be a career derailer or it can be a learning experience that leads to greater leadership capacity. Thomas Edison said, "I haven't failed. I've just found 10,000 ways that don't work." For what failure do you need to forgive yourself? Is there need for apology or restitution? Which member of your team needs the gift of forgiveness?

CHAPTER 33

LEADING FROM ANY CHAIR: SECOND CHAIR HAS INFLUENCE. Do you value the insight of everyone in your organization? Do you acknowledge the importance of their voice? Do you collect the ideas of people in every cubicle and work area in your company? When you do, you have expanded your leadership capacity exponentially! You have an informed number of leaders in your organization who may never have a title, but they are by definition, leaders. They come to work most days and combine influence and action to try to make your company one of the best places to work!

REFLECTIVE QUESTION: When is the last time you wandered around your company with the only agenda of noticing, acknowledging, and listening when you ask: "If you could change anything around here, what would you change?"

CHAPTER 34

FIVE QUESTIONS: WHEN DID YOU LAST ASK...?: Some leaders have the organizational assignment to think strategically about where the company is today and where it needs to be in eighteen or twenty-four months. A personal offsite scheduled on your calendar will provide the time and place to leave operations behind and spend an entire day analyzing the most relevant data. Use the five questions to get started. Spend an hour on each one. Sit, think, look at the hard data, dream, write notes, and then take the remaining hours to draft a strategy reflection. This is not a strategic plan, but it is strategic thinking. Perhaps it is only a list of observations in response to each of the five questions. Those observations will contribute to the effectiveness and efficiency of achieving your productive potential!

REFLECTION QUESTIONS: What if you could invest minimal time and resources to increase your leadership capacity by 5 percent. Would you do it? The *D.W.Y.S.Y.W.G.T.D.* acronym is impossible to pronounce, so just consider the words: *Do What You Said You Were Going to Do!* When will you ask the five questions? When will you guide your team to ask the questions? Will you let them answer with their authentic perspective?

CHAPTER 35

NINE BOX REVISITED: PERFORMANCE, POTENTIAL, AND PERSONAL DRIVE. The leadership assignment is not to level the playing field. Actually, we must all admit that the playing field isn't level. So, accept the reality that team members are at different places in each matrix and work to move everyone toward the upper right.

REFLECTION QUESTIONS: Who is in what section on each matrix? What is your coaching communication strategy for those in each box? How long will you wait to address the development of each team member?

CHAPTER 36

THREE AVENUES: HOW TO EXTEND LEADERSHIP CAPACITY. The best leaders are lifelong learners. They continue to refine the behaviors and skills needed in their current role and any anticipated roles.

REFLECTION QUESTIONS: Do you feel guilty taking time for your professional development as if you are somehow cheating the organization or not doing your job? Do you understand that increasing your competence adds value to the organization?

CHAPTER 37

DELEGATION: THE URGENT AND THE MORE IMPORTANT. Delegation is a *handing off* process combined with a *letting go* process. *Handing off* is an assignment the leader gives to a team member. *Letting go* gives the team member the authority to use time and organizational resources to reach a shared goal. When leaders skip any of the four steps to delegate full responsibility and full authority, it diminishes leadership capacity. The Delegation Return on Investment? The team member gets a stretch assignment that expands their leadership capacity. The leader frees up time and resources to give attention to issues with greater organizational complexity. The organization expands its productive potential.

REFLECTION QUESTIONS: What do you keep doing every week that someone else on your team could do? Is it harder for you to delegate responsibility or to give full authority? If this is difficult for you, what is one small thing you could delegate and truly let go?

CHAPTER 38

NETWORKING: CONNECTIONS LEAD TO NEW TRANSITIONS. Networking is today's investment in tomorrow. Identify who you should be connecting with, both internally and externally. Connections lead to opportunities but also serve as a collection of subject-matter experts you can reach out to at unexpected times of trouble or professional opportunity. The resources at Contacts Count will help you be intentional and focused: www.contactscount.com

REFLECTION QUESTIONS: Who are the five people with whom you should connect within your organization to gain a better comprehensive perspective of your company? Who are the five on your list outside of your company? How will you connect? What will your agenda of questions include?

CHAPTER 39

THE TIES THAT BIND: THE CONFLICT THAT DIVIDES. The seven ties are not complicated or difficult to implement. Every connection between leader and team touches your capacity as the leader as well as the team's productive potential. Stepping into conflict and managing the flow of ideas and conclusions also adds to your capacity by multiplying the conflicting ideas that can lead to an uptick in your productive potential.

REFLECTION QUESTIONS: Which of the seven ties will most strengthen your capacity to lead more effectively and efficiently? Which one is already successful? Which of the four conflict principles will you develop as a new leadership habit?

CHAPTER 40

MAKE TECHNOLOGY WORK FOR YOU: THE AI LEADER. One of the smarter leadership moves you can make is to share the digital learning curve with your executive team. Make digital literacy part of your executive leadership team agenda by having each member lead a specific digital discussion. Perhaps rotate through some aspect of this topic until everyone in the board room feels ownership. Learn together so you can discuss it intelligently and make wise decisions.

REFLECTION QUESTIONS: Do you know what you don't yet know? That's conscious incompetence which is better than unconscious incompetence. Where should you begin?

CHAPTER 41

HARDWIRING NEW LEADERSHIP HABITS: THINK, TALK, ACT, REFLECT. Most have a personal default in preferring one of four approaches to adult learning styles. A holistic approach incorporates all of these steps to let new ways of leading become internalized in a way that expands our leadership capacity. This is when change, growth, and development have the potential to help us achieve our full productive potential.

REFLECTION QUESTIONS: What are you thinking about and learning as a result? What are you talking about and then understanding more? What stretch assignments are you tackling that apply new learning? How are you debriefing what went well and what didn't? Will you consider using the *Hardwiring Leadership Behaviors and Leadership Competencies Worksheet* to create your plan to extend your leadership capacity?

CHAPTER 42

GUARDRAILS: KEEPING LEADERS ON TRACK. Organizations benefit from leaders who are in it for the long haul. The resilience of sustainable leadership is about the ability to adapt to change long before it is too late. It's about leaders who are agile enough to adjust their leadership competency mix in order to transform the organizational culture. It's an important but lofty goal to achieve strategic outcomes while consistently modeling corporate values. It's about the connection of character and competence as you push the limits of your capacity as a leader. It's never too late nor impossible to make changes. Just start with one of the troubling questions above. Start small. Just start.

REFLECTION QUESTIONS: Is your largest effectiveness gap in the area of leadership character or leadership competence? Have you ever tested your capacity through stretch assignments that invite you to close existing gaps between what is and what should be?

EPILOGUE

RESILIENCE: LEADING FOR THE LONG HAUL. Creative staying power increases the odds of making the impossible possible. It will demand every ounce of leadership skill, personal determination, innovative resourcefulness, collaborative effort, emotional intelligence, and physical stamina. Is there *always* a way home and back to normal? Honestly, No. Yet, sustaining leaders will always see an inevitable ending as a new beginning.

REFLECTION QUESTIONS: Where do you fall on the optimism/pessimism spectrum? What is one leadership shortcoming that you need to address to be a better leader? Is it an aspect of character that is tied to positive influence? Is it an area of competence needed in your next steps forward that will contribute to your effective action? When will you do something about it?

END NOTES

PART ONE

THE SHADOW SIDE OF CHARACTER: IS HONESTY THE BEST POLICY

1. Dr. Tessa West, "The Lies We Tell at Work—and the Damage They Do," *Wall Street Journal*, 27 March 2020.

2. Fred Kiel, *Return on Character: The Real Reason Leaders and Their Companies Win*, (Boston: Harvard Business Review Press, 2015).

3. Scott S. Smith, "Quiet Revolutionary Frances Hesselbein Makes Leadership Her Mission," *Investor's Business Daily*, 28 January 2017, access date 28 March 2020, https://www.investors.com/news/management/leaders-and-success/quiet-revolutionary-frances-hesselbein-makes-leadership-her-mission/.

4. The HOW Institute for Society, access date 30 September 2020, https://www.thehowinstitute.org.

5. The Arbinger Institute, Leadership and Self-Deception: *Getting Out of the Box*, (Oakland: Arbinger Properties Inc., 2010).

CHAPTER 6

1. Josephson Institute, access date 25 April 2020, https://www.josephsoninstitute.org.

CHAPTER 9

1. Kenneth Branagh, *Cinderella*, 1950; Burbank: Walt Disney Studio Motion Pictures, 2015.

CHAPTER 10

1. Merriam-Webster, "pecking order," accessed April 10, 2020, https://www.merriam-webster.com/dictionary/peckingorder.

2. Brian Barth, "The Secrets of Chicken Flocks' Pecking Order," 16 March 2016, access date 24 July 2020, https://modernfarmer.com/2016/03/pecking-order/.

CHAPTER 11

1. Joel Trammel, "5 Ways to Discover the Biggest Problems in Your Company," Inc. Com, 16 September 2016, access date 3 August 2020, https://www.inc.com/joel-trammell/5-ways-to-discover-the-biggest-problems-in-your-company.html.

PART TWO

THE SHADOW SIDE OF COMPETENCE: PETER'S PREDICTIVE PRINCIPLE

1. Dr. Laurence J. Peter and Raymond Hull, *The Peter Principle: Why Things Always Go Wrong*, (New York City: Harper Business, 1969)

2. Scott Adams, *The Dilbert Principle: A Cubicle's-Eye View of Bosses, Meetings, Management Fads & Other Workplace Afflictions*, (New York City: Harper Business, 1997).

3. "Driving Performance: How Leadership Development Powers Success," Center for Creative Leadership, access date 13 June 2020,

https://www.ccl.org/articles/white-papers/driving-performance-development-success/.

4. Kevin Sheridan, "*The Business Case for Leadership Development and Learning*," Association for Talent Development, 3 October 2017, access date 15 July 2020, https://kevinsheridanllc.com/2017/10/leadership-development/.

CHAPTER 22

1. Center for Creative Leadership, "4 Reasons to Invest in Leadership Development," access date 4 August 2020, https://www.ccl.org/articles/leading-effectively-articles/hr-pipeline-4-reasons-to-invest-in-leadership-development/.

2. "Healthy Communities Healthy Youth," Search Institute, 1995, access date 22 March 2020, https://www.search-institute.org/our-research/development-assets/developmental-assets-framework/.

CHAPTER 24

1. Peter M. Senge, *The Fifth Discipline: The Art & Practice of the Learning Organization*, (New York City: Doubleday, 2006).

CHAPTER 26

1. Rich Horwath, *Deep Drive: The Proven Method for Building Strategy, Focusing Your Resources, and Taking Smart Action*, (Austin: Green Leaf Group Press, 2009), 28.

CHAPTER 28

1. Jim Collins, *Good to Great: Why Some Companies Make the Leap and Others Don't*, (New York City: Harper Business, 2001), 87.

2. Bill George, *7 Lessons for Leading in Crisis*, (San Francisco: Jossey-Bass, 2009).

3. Bill George, "Leading in Times of Crisis," World Business Forum, 6 October 2009, access date 9 April 2020, https://www.billgeorge.org/page/leading-in-times-of-crisis.

PART THREE

THE SHADOW SIDE OF CAPACITY: CAN? SHOULD I? MUST I?

1. Gallup, *Now, Discover Your Strengths*, (New York City: Gallup Press, 2020).

CHAPTER 30

1. Amy Cuddy, *Presence: Bringing Your Boldest Self to your Biggest Challenges*, New York City: Little, Brown Spark, 2015).

2. The Right Question Institute, access date 24 April 2020, "Questioning is the ability to organize our thinking around what we don't know," www.rightquestion.org.

CHAPTER 33

1. Ben Zander, "The Transformative Power of Classical Music," TED, 2008, access date 4 March 2020, https://www.ted.com/talks/benjamin_zander_the_transformative_power_of_classical_music?language=en.

2. Ben and Rosamund Zander, *The Art of Possibility: Transforming Professional and Personal Life*, (New York City: Penguin Books, 2002).

CHAPTER 36

1. Charles Duhigg, *Power of Habit: Why We Do What We Do in Life and Business*, (New York City: Random House Trade Paperbacks, 2014).

CHAPTER 38

1. Lynda Gratton and Andrew Scott, *The 100-Year Life: Living and Working in an Age of Longevity*, (New York City: Bloomsbury Business, 2017), 95.

2. Anne Baber, Lynne Waymon, Andre Alphonso, and Jim Wylde, *Strategic Connections: The New Face of Networking in a Collaborative World*, (New York City: AMACOM, 2015) 5-8.

CHAPTER 39

1. Roger Fisher, William Ury, and Bruce Paton, *Getting to Yes: Negotiating Agreement Without Giving In*, (London: Penguin Books, 2011).

2. Patrick Lencioni, *The Five Dysfunctions of a Team: A Leadership Fable*, (San Francisco: Jossey-Bass, 2002).

3. David Horsager, *The Trust Edge: How Top Leaders Gain Faster Results, Deepen Relationships, and a Stronger Bottom Line*, (New York City: Free Press, 2012).

CHAPTER 40

1. Michael M. Lombardo and Robert W. Eichinger *FYI: For Your Improvement, A Guide for Development and Coaching*, (Los Angeles: Lominger/KornFerry, 2000).

2. Gerald Kane, "Common Traits of the Best Digital Leaders," *MIT*

Sloan School of Management Review, 9 July 2018.

EPILOGUE

1. Ridley Scott, *The Martian*, Los Angeles: 20th Century Fox, 2015.

2. Martin E. P. Seligman, *Learned Optimism: How to Change Your Mind and Your Life*, (New York City: Vintage, 2006).

AFTERWORD

1. Marshall Goldsmith, "6 Questions That Will Set You Up to be Super Successful," Marshall Goldsmith Blog, 20 July 2015, access date 14 April 2020, https://www.marshallgoldsmith.com/articles/6-questions-that-will-set-you-up-to-be-super-successful/.

INDEX

◆

rumors, 89–90, 304

NOTES